# Make Room
## *Finding Where Faith Fits*

by
Jonathan McReynolds

D1596861

R.H.Boyd
Publishing
~ R.H.Boyd company

R.H. Boyd Publishing Corporation
Nashville, Tennessee

# Make Room
*Finding Where Faith Fits*

R.H. Boyd Publishing Corporation
6717 Centennial Blvd.
Nashville, Tennessee 37209
www.RHBoyd.com

Facebook: @RHBoydPublishing; Twitter/Instagram: @NationalBaptist

First Printing: November 2018

# Contents

# What Others Are Saying About
## Make Room

Just as Jonathan's music has for years, this book gets to the heart of the matter for his generation. *Make Room*, the album and the book, speak to the Christian veteran as well the newest convert. None of us can afford to squeeze God out, and I appreciate Jonathan for beautifully shining light on how we all may do just that.

**Pastor John Hannah**
*New Life Covenant Church, Chicago, Ill.*

• • • • • • •

Our relationship with Jesus only works when we give "space" as an avenue to foster and nurture it. Jonathan McReynolds has captured the essence of this conversation with *Make Room*.

**Jason Nelson**
*Gospel Artist*

• • • • • • •

As you read through this extraordinary reshaping of your God-perspective, don't pass up the invitation to create the necessary space for *God* to be and do all *He* wants to be and do in you and for you.

**Pastor Hart Ramsey**
*Faith Leader, Pastor, Artist, and Author*

• • • • • • •

*Make Room* is a powerful, witty, and riveting challenge to bring Jesus from the edges and outskirts of your life to the most influential centerpoint of guidance and control.

**Pastor Charles Jenkins**
*Award-winning Songwriter and Faith Leader*

• • • • • • •

*Make Room* is not merely a book title, but a call to action for all God's people! *Make Room* is a must have with a message everyone needs to hear!

**Dr. Joseph L. Williams**
*Senior Pastor, Salem Bible Church, Atlanta-Lithonia, Ga.*

# Acknowledgments

O ur firsts are always the most special, so I am aware that there is an innocence, a nervousness, and a freshness that I'll never get back from having my first book published.

I thank "Mrs. New Business" Steph for getting behind the wheel and driving us all here to help me fulfill a dream and begin a new journey. Walter has spearheaded all that is Jonathan McReynolds for a while now and I love you for it, Brother! I'm thankful for LaDonna and the entire R.H. Boyd Publishing family for taking chances, making room.

Mom modeled it first: making room for God in every element of her life. I'm thankful for her and the many models I've come across in this business. The industry gets a bad rap for not making much room for God, but that's just because many haven't met William, Travis, Tasha, Anthony, Jason, Natalie, Hart, John, Jenkins, Phil and EJ yet! Thank you for showing me what God can do with room! Thank You, God, for the many mirrors You've given me, human or otherwise, simply to show me I was squeezing You out.

Thank you, Pastor Jackson and Pastor Hannah, for keeping me fed while I walk through this wilderness of music ministry. Love you, New Original and New Life!

God bless every friend and every family. You're always in mind as I write songs and stories. I pray I've made you proud!

# Words from the Publisher

*W*ith **Make Room:** *Finding Where Faith Fits*, Jonathan McReynolds gives readers a handbook on how to create space for God in every aspect of their lives. We all must make room for a daily investment in our walk with Christ, and we must perform daily calibration with His Word and plan for us. A Sunday worship experience is not enough to carry us through our faith walk. We must die to self daily... surrender to Christ daily.

We cannot compartmentalize Christ and save Him for the occasions when we are in church—Sunday worship service or Wednesday Bible study.

Jonathan encourages us to make room for God everywhere in our lives, every day of our lives because "Why we fight is often why we die, why we smile, and why we cry" (p. 56).

None of us are perfect; however, we serve a God who is without fault or failure. As Jonathan wrote, we must "...speak from a place of pursuit, rather than mastery" (pg. 18). We will never master what it means to be a perfect example of Christianity, and fortunately, that is not the expectation. Little by little, day by day, we can get closer to our ideal selves. We must strive to create "A lifestyle based on what makes room for God to move, bless, teach, and challenge [which] is pleasing to Him and is rewarding and enlightening to us because it places Christ at the center" (pg. 131).

We are pleased to partner with Jonathan to release this forthright and engaging book. We also are grateful for the opportunity to be a strong voice in Christian publishing for five generations. Since 1896, we have provided resources for those seeking to deepen their faith walk with Christ, and we take great pride in being storytellers of the African-American experience from a faith perspective.

LaDonna Boyd
*President/CEO*
*R.H. Boyd Publishing Corporation*

# Foreword

**R**eading is not my favorite thing to do. I actually can list ten other things I'd rather do: video games, basketball, hanging with the wifey, and seven other things I'm sure I'd find more interesting than picking up a book. What makes my honest confession ridiculous is that after eighteen years of school, I know how powerful reading is. It seems that anything that's good for me is often a struggle. Spinach stands no chance against banana pudding. My fingers scroll through IG stories much more than through Paul's letters.

One day, I pushed past my fun list and read an interesting story about a hotel manager. There was a big conference in town and the rooms were filling up fast. Like on the TV show *Undercover Boss*, the conference organizer came in disguise and attempted to book a room. The hotel manager lost a major opportunity to be promoted by closing his doors on the undercover special guest. The Guest and His family ended up staying with animals, and thirty-three years later He saved humanity.

When I take a serious look at the daily distractions that I embrace, I'm more like the hotel manager than the desperate shepherds who chased stars in order to get a glimpse of the Messiah. The invitation to make room is an offer that has been extended since His birth. What the religious weren't willing to do in His lifetime, He accomplished in His death. In essence, He said, "Since you won't make room for me, I'll make it for you."

The place of separation between God and humanity was the Holy of Holies, but like a stage director revealing the set design, God opened the veil of His temple, making room for us once and for all.

Jonathan's *Make Room* is refreshingly honest. Even for someone like me who avoids books like a treadmill, I was hooked from the first line. The wisdom and revelation painted on these pages could only come from someone who has spent time with God. Jonathan's courageous transparency exposes and eliminates every argument of why we've reserved only two out of 168 hours each week for God's presence.

You hold in your hands this generation's manual for proper priority alignment. If there's no vacancy, don't be like the hotel manager; kick something out and make room!

Get ready! God is drawn to empty spaces.

Travis Greene, *Gospel Artist*

" I find space for what I treasure.
I make time for what I want."

"Make Room"
*Make Room*

## Opening Thoughts
## Make Room

"**o, you're writing** a book huh?" My godmother prodded. (One of my greatest supporters, she is still adjusting to my transition from "Jonatin," the nerdy, church organist, to this public minister, Jonathan.) "What's it about?"

I liked my answer. "You know...just trying to give Jesus another place to live."

Allowing Jesus to live some place other than church is a new idea for some, even for believers. Contemporary Christianity has unwittingly taught us that Jesus lives at church, so we tend to just leave Him there. We acknowledge our identity as believers and we claim our Christian religion no matter where we go. But we tend to embrace Him zealously in church and then cease to embrace Him like that again until we return.

He's used to it, though.

His earthly parents, Mary and Joseph, had some "good church" in Luke 2:43, but then accidentally left Jesus at the Temple. They assumed He was somewhere among the crowd in their caravan of travelers, possibly tagging along with some other friends and family, so they weren't intentional about maintaining firsthand contact with Him. I can only imagine someone said, "Hey Mary, where's your Jesus?" The family made a U-turn to Jerusalem and found Him in the temple demonstrating His genius. He was doing just fine. Jesus loved hanging out in the church of His day. It was the folks charged with keeping up with Him—and failing at it—that lost their peace. Even now Jesus does not lose His integrity when you leave Him at church; but your faith gets unsettled. Your status and power as a Christian flip flops. And somewhere in the middle of your road rage, lusting, hating, cussin' spree someone ought to ask, "Hey, where's your Jesus?"

"Oh yeah, let me turn around."

## Claustrophobia

We have highly contradictory expectations of God. We expect Him to protect us from the consequences of our bad choices—even if we failed to include Him in the decision-making process. He's supposed to give us a pleasant and fulfilling life, even if the way we've lived has little to do with God at all. We expect Him to lead us to marriage, but we don't bother to pray about who we date. We pray that He boosts our career, when we don't have Kingdom-minded plans regarding the money we would make. Contrary to what Matthew 6:3 says, we still

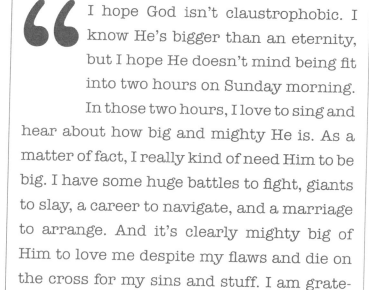
I hope God isn't claustrophobic. I know He's bigger than an eternity, but I hope He doesn't mind being fit into two hours on Sunday morning.

In those two hours, I love to sing and hear about how big and mighty He is. As a matter of fact, I really kind of need Him to be big. I have some huge battles to fight, giants to slay, a career to navigate, and a marriage to arrange. And it's clearly mighty big of Him to love me despite my flaws and die on the cross for my sins and stuff. I am grateful that God is so large. But like a twelve-foot Christmas tree stuffed in a room with an eight-foot ceiling, I hope He doesn't mind crouching down. And He'd better be sticking to His code that my gift will make room for me (Prov. 18:16), even though I probably won't make too much more room for Him."

– Someone You Know

expect God to give us what we want without us first seeking the Kingdom and all His righteousness.

*"But seek first his kingdom and his righteousness, and all these things will be given to you as well"* (Matt. 6:33, NIV).

Now, God could be more aggressive and just force us to give Him our full attention. And sometimes I wish He would just do that. "Jonathan! Make more room for Me or I'll smite thee!" Instead He's chosen to "stand at the door and knock," usually only doing what we give Him room to do in our lives. He doesn't force His way in; we have to be open to letting Him in. But people have always been that way—wanting and needing a touch from Him, but refusing to expand their faith to let Him in.

That's what happened when Jesus returned to the town where He grew up. Jesus loved to perform miracles, but when He went back to Nazareth, He was hindered from doing all He could for the people who'd known Him since He was just a boy. Why? Well, the Nazarenes had lots of familiarity with their hometown boy and lots of knowledge, but they also had no faith and no honor, which gave Him no room. Others were praising Him throughout Galilee, but when He got to Nazareth, He walked into a wall of unbelief. They were curious and went to church to hear Him but were not willing to change their thinking, and their lives, for Him. *"Then they scoffed, 'He's just a carpenter, the son of Mary and the brother of James, Joseph, Judas, and Simon. And his sisters live right here among us.' They were deeply offended and refused to believe in him"* (Mark 6:3, NLT).

The Nazarenes' reaction to Jesus proved that regular worship attendance doesn't validate or invalidate your faith. The townspeople went to the synagogue often, but they were unwilling to make room for Jesus and believe that He was capable of doing miraculous things.

It's interesting that when you ask someone, "Are you a Christian?" their answer usually has something to do with church attendance. If they go a lot, they feel like a Christian for sure and answer with confidence. If they don't go regularly or at all, they tend to feel a little less secure about their salvation.

Making room for God means so much more than how often you go to church or whether you even go at all. It is the room that you give God to operate in your life. Making room means giving God space to work in and through your life—the time, energy, and identity you allow Him to use, challenge, and redeem to make a difference in the world. Don't get me wrong! I wish the whole world went to church and I encourage you to consume all the sermons, songs, and Christian fellowship that you can. Even further, I encourage you to help the Church carry out its mission in the community with your time, your talent, and your tithe. But saying that, I have also realized the inadequacy of a church service-based faith and a church service-based relationship with God. Truly making room for God extends further into your life, into every crack and fold.

So, if making room is about more than going to church, why does it seem like people get healed only at loud church revivals? And why do people dance and cry only during worship on Sunday morning? I figure that we have these emotional breakthroughs and charismatic encounters at church because that's the one place where we yield and give God room to inspire those experiences in us. From Monday through Saturday, however, we tend to rely on our own understanding—barely praying, barely listening to God-themed music, ignoring the millions of sermons available on YouTube®, and avoiding the friends who want God, too. So the rest of the week produces drama, stress, and mood swings instead of the fruit of the Spirit. God wants to be our Living Water for nutrition; but instead, we make Him our medicine, just for the sake of repair, until we feel strong enough to do it on our own again. God's power never wavers; however, the amount of space—attention, faith, trust, and patience—we give Him to show that power frequently falters.

Imagine a friend asked you to stay with them for the week. You get to their home and junk is everywhere—nothing is in the fridge, no spare towels are in the bathroom, and there's no clear spot for you to rest at night. You're their friend, so you know they've been busy and maybe their invitation was so spontaneous that they had no time to prepare. Fine. But what if, instead of clearing the junk, planning a grocery run, throwing some bath towels in the laundry, and clearing out the guest room, they just sat down and started watching TV. They invited you, but then they made no effort to make their space livable for you. I imagine you'd even help them straighten up if they asked, but as soon as the door closed behind you, they went back to living their same junky life, as if you had never come.

Well, yeah, we tend to do Jesus like that.

We invite Him in and beg Him to come into our homes (hearts). It's cluttered and unkempt, as He expected. He plans to help us clean up anyway, but as soon as our tearful invitation is accepted and He walks in, we put our feet up and forget that He's there. I wonder if He just stands at the door, perplexed and wondering if we will ever offer Him a seat. As the years roll by, we wonder why His presence hasn't made any drastic changes in and for us. Well, He's probably still standing inside the door, bringing light to the entryway but unable or unwilling to press any further into our neglected mess. His Spirit will help us clean up—in a miraculous, strong, and incredibly effective way—but He won't make us clean up, especially if we don't even acknowledge His presence but a couple of hours a week.

The beauty of Christianity is not just that it offers God souls to save, but also that it provides God a new place to live—in us, with us, and through us. We don't just benefit because Jesus has come into our lives. We benefit because He desires to stay all week long—not just on Sunday. That is, if we have made room for Him to stay. Then, as He takes up residence inside, He tours the house, bringing light and peace, wisdom and healing—but most of all redemption—to every space He's allowed to enter.

"God, here are my thoughts and beliefs. What do You think? Okay, well what about these ambitions and goals that I have? And after this I want to show You my social life. But just get comfortable. It's all Yours."

This is our prayer; for the health of our souls, the trajectory of our lives, and the benefit of our faith depend on our willingness to make room for God.

## Hi, I'm Captain Do-Too-Much

My friends will tell you, that I tend to do too much. Too many events, too many endeavors, too many dates, too many shows, and too many tasks. Yet in that flurry of activity, what I really needed...well, I just didn't seem to have time for. As my blood pressure elevated, and my face broke out (even worse than normal), and I began to consider drinking, I realized that I needed to learn, or re-learn, how to consistently make room for God.

It felt like—and still feels like—my life depended on it.

For whatever reason, God has created me to teach while I yet learn my own material and to speak from a place of pursuit rather than mastery. I'm convicted while I'm singing, and I've been convicted by writing this book. Maybe God knew that if no one else could get through to me, I could.

The getting through process began in 2016. As the year unfolded, a familiar cloud formed over my head. The looming task of writing another album—one that was better than the last—began to unsettle me. There were high expectations from the label and maybe even some of you. My management reminded me of how significant my next body of work would be for my life and my career as an artist. And then, my management team unraveled. I was on my way to the Grammy Awards (for the previous album) knowing I would have to lose graciously. I was fresh off my first sold-out show in London. I was navigating a *situationship*—that is, the weird space between being a friend with a woman but not fully committing (stop judging me) to the relationship. Then there were eighty shows I was scheduled to perform and countless interviews and some television appearances. I bought my first property, launched my nonprofit organization, and dealt with more dates, more drama, more lessons, more failures and misunderstandings, and more stressing about what people thought about me. Oh yeah, and a Dove Award.

Just a lot!

Notice that in my recall of vigorous activity I didn't mention any special moments with God. Looking back, I don't think during that time that there was much consultation, much prayer, much private time, much church service, or much of anything of spiritual value going on in my life! My ministry was taking off because of His promise, but the minister was slowly dying beneath the pressure. I was bound—whether contractually, socially, or financially—to this crowded life. Peace, joy and security were now buried under piles of people, appointments, and to-do lists. I was repaying God for all the room He'd made for me by keeping my spiritual space cluttered.

## The Tale of Two Worlds

Let me back up.

Growing up, I lived a block away from my local church, and it was sort of a second home for me. I never had that rebellious, "I hate church" phase. At most, I just didn't always feel like waking up early for Sunday school. Regardless, my friends and I were all musicians at 11:00 a.m., customers at the corner store at 2:00 p.m., church yard athletes at 3:00 p.m., girl chasers at 5:00 p.m., and then church musicians once again at 7:00 p.m. for the night service. I loved my church boy Sunday itinerary.

> **SECULAR** / sek yə lər/ denoting attitudes, activities, or other things that have no religious or spiritual basis.

But then I went to school the next day where we listened to Nelly and Eminem. I cussed—admittedly, reluctantly—just because that was our language. We were girl-crazy all day, making jokes about stuff we knew nothing about. We weren't old enough to do too much demonstrable sinning; but if we could, we would have. I got no love from the fellas for being a church boy. As a matter of fact, that conversation rarely even came up.

My two worlds never collided. Even on my birthdays, I remember there was a get-together for the school friends, but then a sleepover for the church buddies. I don't think I separated the two groups on purpose. I just thought that's how it should be. Two different cultures; two different value systems. I made room for godly things at church functions and around church folks but there was no room for Jesus apart from those occasions. I carried that approach of compartmentalizing Christ all the way into college. And until I learned to integrate Him into normal life, I was limiting what He could do in my life...just like the Nazarenes.

I allowed Him to help me with church music; but He could have no part of my homework. He was important to me and my church girlfriend, but His name never came up once I got to school. He could wipe away tears on Sundays without getting to influence what caused me to shed tears during the rest of the week. I limited His jurisdiction in my life because I did not make room for Him.

Of course, I know that God can override my assignments and my compartmentalizations whenever He wants. I believe He watched over me during those days, ordered some of my steps, and provided necessary guidance in spite of me. He knew I was young and dumb—but believers can't stay young and dumb. The grace of God can carry us for a time, but at some point, the training wheels have to come off, even if we ride with a few wobbles on the journey.

If I don't yield, if I don't ask, and if I don't make room for Him in the areas beyond the church's walls, there's a good chance He won't intervene. For Christians, the two worlds must collide. There is no such thing as a secular life for a Christian unless you really don't want God to be there. Unless you really don't want unmerited favor, omniscient protection, and peace that surpasses understanding for all seven days of the week.

We learn how to separate God from the rest of life early in our spiritual development. But no attitude, no activity, and no element of your life should be without a religious or spiritual basis—a faith infused, God-led foundation. There is a Christian basis for posting online, relating to your boss, submitting to your teacher, honoring your mom and dad, performing on your job, and appropriating your talent and money. The Holy Spirit, your God-given Counselor and Comforter, is quite concerned with everything that goes on in your life. I'd call it being "nosey," but my mom wouldn't like that. Let's just say He wants to be in everything that has to do with your life. In truth, God has at least permitted everything that happens in your life; but when it comes to His people, He'd prefer your life be full of things He has ordained. His goodness, His values, His standards, and His goals always must be foremost in your heart and mind, even if you can't hear His voice in your ear.

So, first let's deal with that mind of yours!

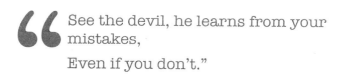 See the devil, he learns from your mistakes,

Even if you don't."

"Cycles"
*Make Room*

## Chapter One
# Make Room...*In Your Head*

**I**'**ve been in** church all my life, so I have heard 2 Corinthians 10:4 read, preached—screamed—hundreds of times. I had no clue what a stronghold was at the time, though. I assumed the verse pointed to our supernatural ability to loosen the grip of the enemy. Like maybe the devil's big hands had a strong...hold...on our wrists...ankles? Something. So instead of just loosening the grip we could, like, destroy his hand altogether.

Not really.

*"For the weapons of our warfare are not of the flesh but have divine power to destroy strongholds."*

*(2 Cor. 10:4, ESV)*

A stronghold is like a fortress, a wall, an extra layer of protection against attack. It reminds me of the kind of snowball fights I read about in books where players could hide behind big walls of snow in between throws. We weren't that sophisticated in the 'hood. We had nothing to protect us from a snowball invasion. But in biblical times, when kings and warriors were under attack, they could hide themselves and their ammunition in these strongholds, guarded from any external harm. Strongholds can be a place of safety for all who run to them.

When Paul spoke of strongholds, he was referring to ideas, doctrines, and beliefs that probably sounded reasonable, but yet were unbiblical, ungodly, or just not God's will for us. These strongholds do not provide safety for us; but rather, safety for the enemy. A Christ-transformed mind is on constant guard against the enemy's attempts to gain a greater footprint in our lives. Even when we are careful in guarding our minds, we often manage to hold on to some thoughts and beliefs, even when the Bible rails against them. In hanging onto that belief, a stronghold is built where the enemy infiltrates and hides until he can find a strategic opportunity to attack. So, in those stubborn strongholds, the enemy is safe from complete eviction, and strategically waits for an opportunity to make your thoughts peace-, trust-, joy-, and most of all, faith-destroying.

I'm sure you can think of several reasonable—humanitarian even—ideas and standards that Christians hold onto, even after declaring faith in and surrendering to Christ. Some strongholds are sexual. Some are racial. Others can be financial, nutritional, political, religious, psychological or social. Some of us will give up time, talent, and treasure for the cause of Christ, yet we hold on for dear life to our ideas, even if the Bible or the Holy Spirit reveals something different. Entire denominations and theologies may have been created around stronghold beliefs.

These days, people feel like Christianity is only credible if it already agrees with them: that is, their thoughts on stewarding money; their dreams, ambitions, and career goals; their understanding of gender fluidity; or their perspectives on economics and policy. Everyone is hell-bent on asserting what is right, but not terribly concerned with finding out what truly *is* right. Let me say that one more time. Don't be hell-bent on asserting, tweeting, posting, hashtagging, or arguing what is right and not have that same level of enthusiasm to find out what actually is revealed in God's Word and by the Holy Spirit.

Strongholds sometimes have a way of infiltrating our belief system in a manner that makes them appear benign. Here are some common strongholds I've heard or have wrestled with often. I won't completely answer or address them; instead, I challenge you to pray and study those that you know are built up like mighty, stone castles in your mind.

- *"The Bible isn't relevant anymore."*
  From that, the enemy gives you grounds to question the laws, morals, and the uncomfortable standards that the Bible sets forth. If you can be convinced that God's Word isn't 100 percent God breathed or is inapplicable to today's world, the Bible becomes downgraded to a form of Greek or Roman mythology...and poof... there goes your faith, identity, and pursuit of His righteousness.

- *"I can't believe God would send good people to hell."*
  I had to examine my idea of what's good versus the biblical idea of good. God wants us to be good people. Characteristics like agreeable, genial, generous, resilient, friendly, and compassionate are all traits that I know God wants us to possess. Many of us have some or all of them. But every human being is capable of displaying some not-so-positive traits—like selfishness, pride, anger, brokenness, insecurity, and hostility. Take my word for it, we do not want salvation to be a merit-based opportunity! None of us is so good that we don't have sinful ways. In other words, we can't earn our way into heaven because for every good thing we do, there's another column stacked with negative behaviors and attitudes. Strongholds built on the belief that some people are too "good" to go to hell can threaten your faith. Every time a beloved non-believer dies, every time you realize how many people aren't followers of Christ, and every time you grow a friendship with someone outside of the faith, you're tempted to hang on to this stronghold.

- *"The Church shames some sins and ignores others."*
  Standing behind this stronghold, we set up church folks as our greatest enemy and judge of our actions when maybe it's God. We use the sins of others to substantiate, magnify, or even diminish our own. Or even worse, the enemy will make us believe the commonness of a certain sin within culture makes it a lesser a sin or not an issue at all. But the plain fact is that God has laws and

rules by which humanity is called to live—whether we like it or not, whether somebody else likes it or not, and whether the rest of the world is doing it or not.

- *"God knows my heart."*
  The strongest strongholds aren't just your thoughts, but also thought patterns governed by guilt, bad habits, attachments to ungodly people, unworthiness, fear, anger, or perceived inability to connect with God. (This is particularly problematic when a relationship with God is defined as those kinds of charismatic experiences that everyone doesn't seem to have.) It's not enough that God knows you have good intentions. Your actions matter, and the ones that go against Him are called sin, plain and simple.

Making room in your mind also means cleaning out the negative thoughts that can hold you back from even trying to do something great for God. The enemy can build strongholds of doubt, guilt, low self-esteem and fear in your head to convince you that you have no business trying to play a role in God's work on earth. "Ministry? That's for those people who haven't done the things I've done. God's got somebody better than me to do His work."

That's how we get held up from making room for God. Our lives get filled with negative thoughts about who we are, what we've done, and what we are capable of doing for God's Kingdom.

You may already know the story of how the Israelites made it to the Promised Land. Joshua, the man who led them there, is one of the most intriguing personalities of the Bible. God gave him and his generation the awesome task of moving Israel into Canaan, the Promised Land, after forty years of wandering in the wilderness. Now, when Joshua took his men over the Jordan River and they set their feet in Canaan, the first combat they had to fight was the Battle of Jericho. The city was impregnable because there were walls that protected the city. And the Bible says (Joshua 6:1) that the gates of Jericho were kept shut and guarded to keep the Israelites out. No one could enter or leave the city. In the Bible such cities are known as strongholds.

Not only do nations have cities that are strongholds, like Jericho, but there are strongholds in our lives also. We all have some Jerichos. We all have some impregnable fortress, something in our way, preventing us from possessing our Promised Land.

Bad habits and bitter feelings are perfect building blocks to erect strongholds. Low esteem, self-deprecation, and holding on to past failures—strongholds. Many of us have set up a lively worship tent next to our stronghold; nevertheless, we have become comfortable with it being there. So, we try to create loving relationships, but a stronghold of hurt or abuse won't let love come in. Some of us are bent on self-destruction because of a stronghold that won't let the truth of their worth in. See how the enemy stays safe from complete eviction and you stay blocked from complete occupancy.

Whether the stronghold is from our thinking or from our doing or from something beyond our control, it has to be brought down so that space can be filled with His presence. Ravi Zacharias, quite the biblical scholar and apologist, asserted in an audio book, *Lessons from War in a Battle of Ideas* (Ravi Zacharias International Ministries, 2000):

> A commanding officer coming onto the beach issued orders to one of his captains...When asked to attack one of the houses and take it, the captain, full of fear, said to his commanding officer "I do not know how to take a building like that."...The captain was quite skilled in handling the open spaces, the big beach areas, but he did not know how to capture one small building in which there was enough firepower to destroy them....So much of our study has been to enable us to take some of the open spaces, the masses, when many have been left untrained in how to take the strongholds and bastions where ideas that are antithetical to the Gospel reign.

(BTW, Ravi's discussions on the defense and "proof" of our faith may offer some answers to your questions.)

Paul's words in 2 Corinthians 10:4 should comfort all believers about their strongholds. There he says we have access to divine Power that can destroy the strongholds that are built and maintained in the body of Christ—the strongholds that invite division and demonic oppression. You know what it will take to obtain this power? Making room for God to change your mind, and sometimes your circumstances, too.

## Carrying Too Much

I'm the type of guy who doesn't like making two trips with groceries. No matter how many bags there are, most of the time I figure out a way to carry them all at once. Normally, I can get about six bags on the middle three fingers per hand, one precariously hanging on each pinky finger, and one more tucked underneath each arm. This is an especially amazing feat when I go to the grocery store on my way home from the airport because some of these "bags" are heavy luggage cases.

After I get them all in hand, I take a moment to adjust, nudge the car door closed, and proceed to my gate. Something quite deflating happens there, though. The cumbersomeness and the weight of the bags make it impossible to lift up my arm, negotiate the keys, and get the right one into the lock. The ridiculous load is manageable outside, but if I want to go in, I almost always have to drop, even if only for a moment, some of that heavy baggage.

Jesus called to all the "heavy laden," so coming out of darkness with baggage is normal, but to fully go into the marvelous light, expect to drop some ideas, beliefs, and convictions until you are sure you can go in with them. Some of your thoughts may be confirmed and appreciated so you can pick them back up, but some ideas just cannot make this trip. The same goes for people, but we can talk about that later.

## Hoarders

When Romans 12:2 (NKJV) says, *"Do not be conformed to this world, but be transformed by the renewing of your mind,"* did you really expect your current world views and truths to not ever be challenged? It says transformed, not affirmed.

And if you really want to live in the fullness and power of the faith, there likely are some thoughts and thought patterns that you and God must throw out.

One of the most entertaining, but troubling shows I've watched is called *Hoarders*. It's like an hour-long car wreck. I guess thousands of people around the country don't know how to throw stuff away. I mean some stuff is clearly trash and rotten; nevertheless, they have a strange attachment to it. Subjects often live amongst feces, mold, and rodents because they hoard a breeding ground of junk. Some of it's junk that may have actually been valuable once, but now is ruining their lives.

Sometimes it's kind of uncomfortably funny—the ridiculousness of it—but it takes a saddening, sobering turn when you realize their loved ones, even their kids, are driven away simply because there is no safe space for them to engage. Much of the time, the hoarder is embarrassed, but fairly content in his or her mess, but they are certainly the only ones willing to live there! If you want to continue in this life autonomously and lean on your own merit, hold on to your ridiculous hoarding ways; it's your prerogative. If you want God to dwell with you, though, it's time to clear out some old thoughts. Like a good Hoarders-certified organization specialist, God's Word and God's people can help, holding up one unfit thought at a time, thus letting you decide if you just really need this mess in the new, cleaner life you profess to want. Know that every bit of residue, however, makes it more likely you'll make another pile of mess as soon as the crew leaves.

Let's make some room in our heads. Do you have some thoughts, beliefs, and habits that may not be fit for the ex-hoarder version of you? I know I did before and still may. If you promise you'll think about it, I'll try to list some of the ideas I have needed—and still need—to check with God about. I repeat: these are not answers and conclusions, nor are they necessarily concerns that you should have yourself. This is simply my list of thoughts, concerns and questions for which I must intentionally give God room to give me understanding and transformation.

- I like bacon. And the occasional pork chop. And eating a lot. Quickly. Is that best for my temple? Does it offend God? Break any laws?

- I don't drink, but some of my friends do. That's cool, right?

- So once and for all, is homosexuality a straight up sin and should I be laying down the law (unsolicited) to people who identify with it? If so, how?

- Do I need to be at church every week, and isn't tithing one of those Old Testament things?

- Who made up curse words anyway?! Can't I say them sometimes? It really helps me get the point across.

- My brother-in-law committed suicide, could he have possibly gone to heaven?

- Evolution claims to be the more scientific explanation of how we got here, so what's that "on the fifth day" business in Genesis?

- I'm from the Southside of Chicago! I'm not turning another cheek for nobody!

- Once saved, always saved.

- Men don't cry and some of the things they expect you to do in church are kind of girly and soft.

- When it comes to your dreams, it is better to walk ahead in faith rather than wait on God.

- Gospel music is cool for some occasions, but I need a few more genres (90's R&B, hip hop, country, and pop) in my life. I promise not to internalize the lyrics, let them change me, or whatever, but...

- All that shouting, dancing, rolling, tongue speaking stuff? Does it really take all that?

- Holiness or hell, right? Either you live pursuing and just missing perfection, or you're totally screwed.

- I'm not a huge people person. Do I have to smile and talk to folks at church or anywhere else?

- God blesses, and therefore, loves some people more than He loves me. And me more than some people.

- God made me a Virgo, right? Horoscopes just seem so accurate sometimes.

Can you relate? Some ideas I could keep. Some I had to tweak. Some held truth but the heart behind it was all wrong. Some were just all wrong. If you're looking for me to answer some of these things for you, I'll write another book...but you're missing the point. God wants you to take it to Him, His Word.

I had to give God room—honest room—to transform my mind. You do, too!

I do research and study the scriptures on those subjects until I can have peace. I've had to ask God to help me understand the craziness that happens in church. It feels like a circus sometimes. And I'm learning how to give grace and mercy to folks that I don't think deserve it. To paraphrase what former first lady Michelle Obama said, "When they go low, I've got to go high," but I also must resist the urge to drop stuff from the sky. And if God was willing to die for me, I should be willing to smile a little bit more at someone else. I know that the Bible has the universal truth for believers, but as I make more room for Him, I find that some standards are *just for me*!

In the book of Judges, Samson's parents were given explicit instructions that he was to be reared as a Nazirite, which meant he was not permitted to do things may have been acceptable for other people. He was a supernaturally strong man whose power came from his long hair. When his lover Delilah finally cajoled him to reveal the secret to his brawn, she cut his hair and he lost his strength. So, Samson, short hair is not a sin, but you? Don't you touch that mane! God has a tailored mind-renewal plan for you and it coincides with your upbringing, your purpose, and your personality—but you must make room for it.

I beg of you, please make room.

Western culture is in the stronghold-making business. It's how a generation of Christians could promote chattel slavery and use the Bible as justification. It's how another generation can participate in violent racism; how another can normalize sexual immorality; and how still another will allow scientific advances to invalidate their faith. These big castles of faulty, self-serving, egocentric, world-loving, insecurity-driven ideas make room for the enemy as he works to make our minds and our churches uninhabitable for Christ, love, and godliness.

Take some time to write out some of your ideas and beliefs that may not jibe with the Word and the Spirit of God. Note how many times you say or think "I'm a Christian but..." Is it your language, your actions, and your reactions that determine what is sin and what isn't? Subject those possible strongholds to the divine power that can destroy them.

Humble yourself.

None of those intellectual or emotional attachments are worth missing God over.

## Start by Making Room for His Word

IMHO, the first impediment to mind transformation for our generation of believers is that—get this—we don't read the Bible. If this book does nothing else, I hope it moves you to put it down often and pick up the Good Book. We debate God's position without really knowing what He has said. We claim things as God's will, God's voice, and God's movement without ever checking His Word for confirmation.

Make room for the Word of God in your day, every day. In reading His Word, you will find there are often very clear "duh" moments of truth that society has found a way to muddy. There are scriptures that we regularly misquote, confuse with hymns and old songs or sayings, causing us to miss important realities and principles.

Some people have no idea how Ecclesiastes 9:11 really ends. *"The race is not to the swift, nor the battle to the strong..."* (ESV). Check it out. Ecclesiastes itself is full of things we'd normally look to Oprah, Dave Ramsey or end-of-the-movie Morgan Freeman to say. The first method of attack on these pesky strongholds? Scripture. Use it so you don't get confused.

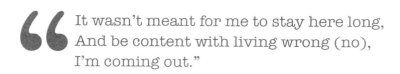

It wasn't meant for me to stay here long,
And be content with living wrong (no),
I'm coming out."

"Comin' Out"
*Life Music*

## Chapter Two
# Make Room...*In Your Dreams and Desires*

*I* **cannot imagine** a more ambitious generation—and by
ambitious I mean a people so in pursuit of success and so
ready to make it happen. And what do I mean by success?
Well, perhaps we can define that later. By age 35, it seems
we all have at least an idea for a nonprofit organization, a
celebrity-sounding social media handle, a failed business, an
idea for a new business, and a strong sense that at least one
hundred jealous "haters" convene somewhere regularly just
to talk against something we haven't even done yet! We all
hope to eventually have enough clout and money to create
"like, a center...where people can learn art, record music,
learn basketball, and breathe in positivity." You've heard
someone say that before, right?

Our ambitions generally are beautiful, but mostly they are
still centered around human issues such as status and legacy.
I wonder how many of us would care to do "big things" if we
were guaranteed that no one would notice. Even the greatest

philanthropists in history are never purely selfless. I'm not even sure humans can be that anyway. Some philanthropists today give to promote a cause they care about. Others give for the tax write-off. Still others give because it makes them feel good. People who have a heart to give usually get an endorphin boost from giving. So even a philanthropist gains something from giving.

The writer of Ecclesiastes, likely King Solomon, says *"I observed that most people are motivated to success because they envy their neighbors"* (Eccl. 4:4, NLT). That's still true today. How many people are driven to attain more because of what they've seen someone else accomplish? How many homes, cars, wardrobes, or even college degrees have been pursued all because someone else has it, too?

God knows us well, though, and can use us even in our selfishness...even despite our selfishness. So even if our motive to succeed is not purely to serve Him, God can still make our success work for His purposes. God can use anyone to accomplish what He wants—a false prophet, a Judas, or even a donkey for that matter. Regardless of a person's motive for doing something, God can direct His will in and through that person's circumstances.

If I can be extra frank for a moment, I'd like to lay a baseline for everything we'll explore in this chapter. No matter how long you have been a Christian or how well you prophesy, you are undeniably God's child and have the Holy Spirit. But you are still human. As such, everything that comes to your mind is not God breathed. Everything you feel is not God's best for you. Everything you desire doesn't have God's stamp of approval on it. Everything you imagine will not manifest in a God-glorifying way, even if you pray fervently for it. We have plans, but God has plans, too. Ultimately, we want His plan to happen and not ours. *"Many are the plans in a person's heart, but it is the Lord's purpose that prevails"* (Prov. 19:21, NIV). Our plans are birthed from wombs of ego, pain, intelligence, observation, external pressure, and creativity, but no matter the source, they must align with God's purpose for us.

That being said, I do not believe that God's will for our lives is a thin balance beam that is easy to fall from. I believe God generally gives us freedom within parameters, but our ears must be directed to His mouth, our eyes focused on His Word, our hearts attuned to His will. When we do this, we can better understand those parameters and His direction for our lives. Then and only then, after we have sought the Kingdom and all His righteousness, can we have what we desire.

In my experience, there are three distinct goals trying to run simultaneously in a Christian's life.

1. *Our temporal, earthly goals.* We want to be married, have kids, start our own profitable business, earn a million dollars, start a church, be famous, become a bishop, write a book, and go to grad school. From these goals, we generate an insane number of short-term plans and choices regarding college, dates, budgets, and time to "sit down and just write." Whether or not we actually get up and accomplish them, we have learned that it is necessary to set high goals for ourselves.

2. *Our actual goals.* These are the objectives we privately, sometimes unconsciously, hope our earthly goals can accomplish. We all have similar human needs but the needs that fail to be met are typically the ones we vigorously pursue as individuals. Our earthly goals generally are dictated by these actual ones—the desires of our hearts. We accomplish various tasks so that we can achieve our heartfelt desires and goals.

Not sure how I got this way, but I've always wanted to be above rebuke. I wanted to do so much good and work so hard that no one could say "He's a bad guy." Turns out, I've since learned that there are a lot of ways you can be labeled a "bad guy." I also learned there is no such thing as a unanimous opinion. So many of my earthly pursuits have been a mad dash to doing something respectable and clearly "good," possibly just to combat some deep feeling of being "bad." I've taken on many tasks and causes—good deeds—in pursuit of my goal of being above rebuke. Who knows? Gangs in my hometown proliferated and are sustained because so many young men desire to be accepted, appreciated, and even celebrated. Being a Gangster Disciple wasn't their real goal, but their real goal drove them to the clutches of the Gangster Disciples.

You may be motivated by a desire to be loved and embraced. That desire may also motivate you to make some choices that are out of God's will. Some people's actual goal is simply to not turn out like their parents.

3.   *God's goal to advance His Kingdom and to draw us into an intimate personal relationship with Him.*

The alignment of these three types of goals is crucial to the success of each. Alignment is critical to attaining fulfillment of what God desires to do in and through us (see Eph. 2:10), the peace that comes from entrusting our lives to Him (Phil. 4:6–7), and the joy of accomplishing His purpose for our lives (Col 1:10–11). The alignment of these goals is the only way the promises of God will ever apply to your goals, desires, and dreams. God will not and should not align with us. Think about how many times you've changed your mind about what you want to accomplish in life. We don't know nothin'! We only perceive what our favorite artist, the preacher at Sunday service, mom, and Hollywood teach us. We have a tough enough time making sense of our present, while God already knows our future. He knows the end from the beginning. His ways are higher than ours and His perspective is complete. We must make room for our goals to align with Him.

So, if true success is what you're after, let me give you a tip: Start with His plan to advance His Kingdom and to draw humanity toward an intimate relationship with Him. Then, everything that He ordains regarding your career, marriage, ministry, and family will direct you toward accomplishing the other two types of goals. If you've written a book that will not advance the Kingdom somehow it will not be established by God. (Even if it's a secular book, those good tithes from your royalties may be used to serve His purpose.) And if the marriage draws you away from Him, God's not a fan of the relationship. Years ago, I asked my friend, renowned worship artist William McDowell, "Are you sure I'm doing what God has called me to do?" It was early in my music ministry and (as with most new artists) I was quite uncertain about everything. William led me down a checklist of scriptures that all amounted to, "Are you and your career choice advancing the Kingdom?" Rather than focus on the creative, the financial, the sentimental, and the political aspects of public ministry, I had to look at my choices honestly and ask whether they were giving God's investment the best return I had to give.

So, be honest: Has God shown you the value of your dreams and aspirations to His grand agenda?

I know you're thinking: What scriptures was William talking about? Here they are, plus a few others that may help:

- *Matthew 28:16–20 (NIV)* – Then the eleven disciples went to Galilee, to the mountain where Jesus had told them to go. [17]When they saw him, they worshiped him; but some doubted. [18]Then Jesus came to them and said, "All authority in heaven and on earth has been given to me. [19]Therefore go and make disciples of all nations, baptizing them in the name of the Father and of the Son and of the Holy Spirit, [20]and teaching them to obey everything I have commanded you. And surely I am with you always, to the very end of the age."

- *Genesis 1:28 (NIV)* – God blessed them and said to them, "Be fruitful and increase in number; fill the earth and subdue it. Rule over the fish in the sea and the birds in the sky and over every living creature that moves on the ground."

- *2 Timothy 2:14–26 (NLT)* – Remind everyone about these things, and command them in God's presence to stop fighting over words. Such arguments are useless, and they can ruin those who hear them. [15]Work hard so you can present yourself to God and receive his approval. Be a good worker, one who does not need to be ashamed and who correctly explains the word of truth. [16]Avoid worthless, foolish talk that only leads to more godless behavior. [17]This kind of talk spreads like cancer, as in the case of Hymenaeus and Philetus. [18]They have left the path of truth, claiming that the resurrection of the dead has already occurred; in this way, they have turned some people away from the faith.[19]But God's truth stands firm like a foundation stone with this inscription: "The Lord knows those who are his," and "All who belong to the Lord must turn away from evil." [20]In a wealthy home some utensils are made of gold and silver, and some are made of wood and clay. The expensive utensils are used for special occasions, and the cheap ones are for everyday use. [21]If you keep yourself pure, you will be a special utensil for honorable use. Your life will be clean, and you will be ready for the Master to use you for every good work. [22]Run from anything that stimulates youthful lusts. Instead, pursue righteous living, faithfulness, love, and peace. Enjoy the companionship of those who call on the Lord with pure hearts. [23]Again I say, don't get involved in foolish, ignorant arguments that only start fights. [24]A servant of the Lord must not quarrel but must be kind to everyone, be able to teach, and be patient with difficult people. [25]Gently instruct those who oppose the truth. Perhaps God will change those people's hearts, and they will learn the truth. [26]Then they will come to their senses and escape from the devil's trap. For they have been held captive by him to do whatever he wants.

- *2 Timothy 1:9 (NLT)* – For God saved us and called us to live a holy life. He did this, not because we deserved it, but because that was his plan from before the beginning of time—to show us his grace through Christ Jesus.

- *2 Peter 1:3-11 (NLT)* – By his divine power, God has given us everything we need for living a godly life. We have received all of this by coming to know him, the one who called us to himself by means of his marvelous glory and excellence. ⁴And because of his glory and excellence, he has given us great and precious promises. These are the promises that enable you to share his divine nature and escape the world's corruption caused by human desires. ⁵In view of all this, make every effort to respond to God's promises. Supplement your faith with a generous provision of moral excellence, and moral excellence with knowledge, ⁶and knowledge with self-control, and self-control with patient endurance, and patient endurance with godliness, ⁷and godliness with brotherly affection, and brotherly affection with love for everyone. ⁸The more you grow like this, the more productive and useful you will be in your knowledge of our Lord Jesus Christ. ⁹But those who fail to develop in this way are shortsighted or blind, forgetting that they have been cleansed from their old sins. ¹⁰So, dear brothers and sisters, work hard to prove that you really are among those God has called and chosen. Do these things, and you will never fall away. ¹¹Then God will give you a grand entrance into the eternal Kingdom of our Lord and Savior Jesus Christ.

- *Mark 10:43 (NIV)* – Not so with you. Instead, whoever wants to become great among you must be your servant,

- *2 Corinthians 5:20 (NIV)* – We are therefore Christ's ambassadors, as though God were making his appeal through us. We implore you on Christ's behalf: Be reconciled to God.

- *1 Thessalonians 2:4 (NLT)* – For we speak as messengers approved by God to be entrusted with the Good News. Our purpose is to please God, not people. He alone examines the motives of our hearts.

- *Ephesians 4:1–16 (NLT)* – Therefore I, a prisoner for serving the Lord, beg you to lead a life worthy of your calling, for you have been called by God. ²Always be humble and gentle. Be patient with each other, making allowance for each other's faults because of your love. [3]Make every effort to keep yourselves united in the Spirit, binding yourselves together with peace. [4]For there is one body and one Spirit, just as you have been called to one glorious hope for the future. [5]There is one Lord, one faith, one baptism, [6]and one God and Father, who is over all and in all and living through all. [7]However, he has given each one of us a special gift through the generosity of Christ. [8]That is why the Scriptures say, "When he ascended to the heights, he led a crowd of captives and gave gifts to his people." [9]Notice that it says "he ascended." This clearly means that Christ also descended to our lowly world. [10]And the same one who descended is the one who ascended higher than all the heavens, so that he might fill the entire universe with himself. [11]Now these are the gifts Christ gave to the church: the apostles, the prophets, the evangelists, and the pastors and teachers. [12]Their responsibility is to equip God's people to do his work and build up the church, the body of Christ. [13]This will continue until we all come to such unity in our faith and knowledge of God's Son that we will be mature in the Lord, measuring up to the full and complete standard of Christ. [14]Then we will no longer be immature like children. We won't be tossed and blown about by every wind of new teaching. We will not be influenced when people try to trick us with lies so clever they sound like the truth. [15]Instead, we will speak the truth in love, growing in every way more and more like Christ, who is the head of his body, the church. [16]He makes the whole body fit together perfectly. As each part does its own special work, it helps the other parts grow, so that the whole body is healthy and growing and full of love.

## Scatter the Salt

I am a proud Chicagoan, but I'll be the first to admit that our weather is not our most attractive feature. They call us the Windy City for a reason. Chicago winters can be brutal.

January mornings often begin with dangerous ice lining our sidewalks, so every prepared household has a bag of salt sitting next to the front door. The idea is that over time each little piece of salt can have its own molecular influence on the cold world around it. Slowly, the pellets of salt soften and melt the surrounding ice.

God has this idea that His disciples, full of his power, can be environment changers. In fact, He tells us that we are salt (see Matt. 5:13). So, when God wants to melt the ice, He has to scatter the salt. He throws out some salt into the medical profession, and into the music industry, and into Hollywood and Silicon Valley. Then He tosses some toward Capitol Hill, the National Basketball Association, and the neighborhood McDonald's®. God disperses His salt, not primarily for us to get promotions and acclaim, endorsements and followers, but to melt the ice!

I know you're working hard to do what you do and to get to where you want to be, but your career is not your primary function in this life. Your primary function is to advance God's Kingdom. But Kingdom advancer just sounds like a weird job title to the world, so God gifts us the capacity to impact the world as an attorney, or manager, or electrician instead. No matter what your career choice, in your head always make room for your real purpose, which is His purpose.

Your real goal has eternal significance. My Instagram® following will be meaningless when a better app comes around, or when everyone stops using apps altogether. No one knows the future, in the near future Instagram may not

Make Room...In Your Dreams and Desires

even be a thing anymore. No human-made thing lasts forever. Honorary street signs eventually rust away. Full nations will be destroyed. But what you do to advance the Kingdom is your lasting legacy.

Like Queen Esther, who rose from obscurity as a Jewish orphan to become queen of Persia, God elevates His people for purposes that serve a greater portion of humanity. After Esther married King Xerxes, something needed to be straightened out to protect the Jews living in Persia. Haman, a nobleman in the court of King Xerxes, wanted to do away with the Jews, and one Jewish man in particular. Haman vowed to kill Mordecai, Esther's adoptive father, and all of his people.

Something had to be done to stop Haman, and Mordecai knew that his beloved Esther was just the person to do it. Initially, Esther was not eager to step up to the plate. She had a lot to lose....not just her crown, but her head along with it.

Esther was able to rise to the level of queen in a land where her status had been just above that of a slave. But this was all a part of God's plan. God positioned Esther to become the next queen and thereby save her people, but she didn't just walk into the blessing of being queen. Esther had been prepared for God to position her in the place where she needed to be to do what He needed her to do.

Esther had moved from obscurity to the royal palace and was living large. She had people waiting on her hand and foot. But God had a greater purpose for her ascendancy. God had elevated Esther for His purpose. Her blessing was to serve a

51

greater good. That's always a gauge for our goals. We should always question whether what we seek from God will bless God and others, as well as ourselves. God elevates us for purposes that are greater than what we can dream of in our own heads. God knew exactly what he was doing when He placed this grain of salt in Xerxes' royal palace.

Today, Queen Esther's royal robes, wherever they may be, are dry rotted, and her jewels and crown are tarnished and lacking their original luster. But what remains is her crown of righteousness. What we have to remember is her testimony of sacrifice to do God's will. The Feast of Purim, the celebration that memorializes her work, lives on.

Jesus warns us, *"Don't store up treasures here on earth, where moths eat them and rust destroys them, and where thieves break in and steal. ²⁰Store your treasures in heaven, where moths and rust cannot destroy, and thieves do not break in and steal. ²¹Wherever your treasure is, there the desires of your heart will also be"* (Matt. 6:19–21, NLT).

## For the Nerds

It is generally my great pleasure to squeeze out everything a metaphor has to offer, and when Jesus refers to believers as "the salt of the earth" in Matthew 5, He most likely was speaking to the general usefulness, stability, and value that salt had during ancient times. Used for flavor, food preservation, healing, and other uses, salt was an important commodity. Personally, however, your boy from Chicago is intrigued by the particular utility of salt in winter. Salt melts ice; but not because it simply heats it up.

Salt changes water on a molecular level, lowering the freezing point at which water can turn to ice. When the salt is present, the temperature that would normally freeze water is no longer low enough. As the salt of the earth, we don't necessarily warm the ice, but our presence makes it a lot harder for the environment to become frozen—completely hardened and numb to the love and truth of God. The enemy must now work harder to harden the hearts of the people around us because the atmosphere has been softened. Water is not so easily compelled to be ice when salt is in the mix. Could it be that our presence as salt alters the nature of ice so that it no longer feels the need to be ice?

## Delight and Desire

*"Delight yourself in the Lord, and he will give you the desires of your heart"* (Ps. 37:4, ESV).

Yo, that's a tricky verse!

Clearly everyone wants their heart's desires, and most people are delighted when they know they are on their way. But I think the verse is often misunderstood and can threaten some people's faith. So many people expect God's gifts to be dictated by their hearts' desires, not realizing that after spending ample time delighting in Him, their desires more closely reflect what He's willing to give.

God is not pumped to give you the car your inflated ego desires. Delight in Him for a while, in awe of His holiness and love. The newly humbled you will want the car for different reasons. And then, He just might give you a private jet.

God is not in a rush to give you a Grammy® so you can stick it to all your haters. Delight in Him, and watch the desires of your heart begin to love your enemies, bless those who curse you, do good to those who hate you, and pray for those who spitefully use you and persecute you (see Matt. 5:44, NKJV). And then He might give you two Grammys.

He doesn't give victims to the murderer, alibis to the liar, and blessings to the boaster. He does, however, give seed to the sower. Make room for Him, and then this promise applies to you:

"Delight yourself in the LORD,
and he will give you the desires of your heart.
  Commit your way to the LORD;
    trust in him and he will act....
Be still before the LORD and wait patiently for him;
    fret not yourself over the one who prospers in his way,
  over the man who carries out evil devices!
  ....those who wait for the LORD shall inherit the land"

(Ps. 37:4–5,7, 9, ESV)

Your actual goals must reflect God's goals. He's not asking you to be perfect. He takes your brokenness and uses it for His purposes, if you allow Him. He seems to relish in using your brokenness to help mend other broken people. God uses broken people every day. When you really think about it, though, we flawed people are all He's got...so He finds a way to use us. Here's some good news: Flaws don't necessarily inhibit our ministry; sometimes flaws are our ministry. He knows how your father's absence from when you were a kid impacts your adult decisions. He knows the societal and religious pressure that has you stressing over being single. He totally gets how you don't want to go to your high school reunion without something to be proud of—a mark of success.

But when He grants us the elevation, the promotion, or the platform we believed Him for, we must be careful not to make that the end of the story. God doesn't elevate us just so that we can live lavishly. He doesn't elevate us just so we can have an expensive car or a bigger house. While there's nothing wrong with having those things, we must make sure that our blessings don't overtake our relationship with the Blesser and His purpose for our lives. God desires that we use our blessings to make a difference in the lives of others and give Him glory.

Our dreams subconsciously make room for our egos, our reputations, and desires. Those dreams must be intentionally reorganized to house our faith and Kingdom agenda.

One of my favorite movies of all time is *Adjustment Bureau*. In the movie, a corporation of men (supernatural beings) make little adjustments in people's lives (e.g. untying their shoe to make them miss a bus) that keep them anchored to the Master Plan established by the Chairman. The protagonist, David Norris, is a troubled but charming man who had a great future in politics; nevertheless, he becomes infatuated with a woman, Elise, who does not fit the Plan. The adjusters work hard to keep Norris from establishing a relationship with Elise. The Chairman knows that her love would fill the deep-seated void in Norris' heart, a void that otherwise would eventually drive him to the White House. Per the Chairman, Norris was destined to be (even needed to be) president.

Eighty sermons could be preached from this movie, but one point it beautifully illustrates is how a lot of human ambition is driven by lack, particularly a lack of self-esteem, validation and love. Even the most confident and self-assured among us secretly hope for a pat on the back or for some applause as an acknowledgment of our success. Few in our generation could live as Jeremiah did, proclaiming the truth with no one really listening, much less applauding. The movie also illustrates how God will sometimes thwart our beautiful plans because they do not align with His plans for us.

Why we fight is often why we die, why we smile, and why we cry.

Human ambition is often rooted in ignoble motivations; it is very important that we make room for God to redeem our dreams just as He has redeemed us. There will be a cost in any career path, but that path will undoubtedly be straighter when our desires become molded to what that God is willing to give us, and not what we hope people—fans, bosses, a spouse, a community, a local church—are willing to give us.

## Room to Work

When God's goals and your actual goals are aligned, the rest gets simple. There is great freedom when everything is not a competition or comparison. You take the pressure off every song you write and every person you date when neither must carry you to your destiny. Earthly goals must be undertaken with great humility and the acknowledgment that God's purposeful outcomes may look pretty random to us sometimes.

*"Now listen, you who say, 'Today or tomorrow we will go to this or that city, spend a year there, carry on business and make money.' Why, you do not even know what will happen tomorrow. What is your life? You are a mist that appears for a little while and then vanishes. Instead, you ought to say, "If it is the Lord's will, we will live and do this or that." As it is, you boast in your arrogant schemes. All such boasting is evil'"* (James 4:13–16, NIV).

*"Invest in seven ventures, yes, in eight; you do not know what disaster may come upon the land. As you do not know the path of the wind, or how the body is formed in a mother's womb, so you cannot understand the work of God, the Maker of all things. Sow your seed in the morning, and at evening let your hands not be idle, for you do not know which will succeed, whether this or that, or whether both will do equally well"* (Eccl. 11:2, 5–6, NIV).

Both passages scream "Spend less time thinking about and proclaiming how you're about to blow the world's mind and more time leaving room for God to blow yours!" If God gave you the vision, there's likely a lot of need for supernatural intervention. There should be a lot of logical wires that are not touching yet. Give God room to work!

We must hold tightly to purpose, but loosely to plans.

More than likely, the goals we have for ourselves as believers are in keeping with what God wants for His people. God wants us to marry—to be fruitful and multiply (Gen. 1:28). He wants us to take on goals that will expand His Kingdom. He wants us to be honest business owners that will render a good service to customers. He wants us to live our best life and use the gifts and talents He has implanted in us. Sometimes the goals we pursue are not so much about the what, but the why. Our earthly goals benefit us and fulfill our desires; but ultimately, all that we strive to do also should glorify God.

What's funny is when we finally make our plans less sacred and inflexible and commit them to the Lord, Proverbs 16:3 says He establishes them!

### Waiters and Walkers

*God, let my words, particularly in this section, fall distinctly on every individual, according to all that is unique in each one.*

There are two biblical approaches this generation tends to take toward goals and dreams: (1) wait on the Lord; and (2) walk by faith. Both are important Christian concepts that must be understood and reckoned with every day, but especially in the area of ambitions, goals, and dreams.

Some people are Waiters. They prefer to wait on the promptings of the Spirit—obvious arrows pointing them to turn left or right. This method works well for people who are sensitive to His voice and can discern the seasons when He's speaking and speaking specifics (and depending on who you ask, that's rarely or all the time). Good Waiters are patient, impressively calm, and constantly trusting in God's sovereignty, timing and provision. However, chronic waiting masks close-mindedness, fear, and stagnation in a person waiting on a "move of God," but not realizing they just might be the move of God themselves! God's blessing doesn't guarantee the road will be easy, and Waiters run the risk of waiting too long to test it.

On the flip side are Walkers, the alpha dog, walk-by-faith-not-by-sight, "Oh, this is gonna happen" folks. They understand that if God said it, He will do it. They know God will bless the work of their hands because they are God's children, right? They make a website, order business cards and flyers, and then pray. They often have remarkable resolve and decision-making power. They believe that God blesses their choices—in relationships, in career decisions, and in everything else. They know that "faith comes by hearing and hearing by the Word of God." Yet sometimes they don't realize that without an authentic Word, these Walkers are really moving by hopes and dreams, rather than by faith. With no Word from God, there was no promise that the business venture would work out, that the album would sell, that the pilot will be picked up, or that the prospective employer would call back.

So, what's a believer to do? Should I wait on the Lord or should I walk by faith? Should I be a Waiter or a Walker?

As usual, the answer is somewhere in the middle. It is the balance of walking and waiting that makes this process of God's unfolding hand in our desires so beautiful, so powerful, but also so demanding of God's daily influence. Consider Moses.

In Exodus 3, God has heard the cries of His people and has decided to come down personally to deliver them. But by personally He means sending Moses. As God speaks, Moses realizes that his little stuttering, Hebrew self will not just be *watching* a move of God; he will *be* a move of God. Then, as Moses walks toward Pharaoh, he's not walking by hopes and dreams; he is walking by faith. He walks to the throne of the Egyptian king based on his having received a Word from God. But even a personal summons from the Lord does not guarantee a journey without bumps on the road.

As Israel's deliverance is in process, the Red Sea presents a huge problem. Moses could have continued to walk straight into the water and drowned a nation in tow. Instead, at a crossroads, he waited on instruction from the Lord. And when the way was made for them on dry land, he began walking again. Throughout their journey to the Promised Land they waited, and they walked. Sometimes they waited more than they walked. Sometimes they walked more than they waited. They walked through the wilderness. They waited for manna from heaven.

For the most part, Moses was a great example of how we must carry the passions and burdens that run intensely through our veins. Moses was as passionate and burdened as anyone in history, but he waited on a Word, proceeded to walk on its foundation, and when met with challenges, he usually humbled himself to wait on further instruction. He messed up when he became more mindful of the earthly goal of a Promised Land and less of the God who would get him there. *"...you betrayed me with the Israelites at the waters of Meribah at Kadesh in the wilderness of Zin. You failed to demonstrate my holiness to the people of Israel there. So you will see the land from a distance, but you may not enter the land I am giving to the people of Israel"* (Deut. 32:51–52, NLT).

The world we live in demands that believers ignore society's pressure to move quickly, and instead wait patiently—meditate patiently—on God's Word. But also, when the world tells us how impossible a challenge is, we must walk boldly in faith—a faith that could only come after hearing something, reading something and studying something directly from Him. The rule is to be in relationship with Him.

I imagine children get frustrated when they are encouraged to have fun, be charismatic, energetic, and unbridled one minute, but patient, calm, and restrained the next. They are cognizant of their feelings, but not of the environment. Like them, I know it's frustrating hearing one preacher say "Wait on the Lord," and another say "Walk by faith." Eventually though, as a child matures in faith, he or she learns which situations call for waiting on God and which call for running wild and pursuing everything for the glory of God. If they eventually learn this then we will, too. Just remain a child of God and you will—I will—learn. Again, the number one "rule" here is to simply be in active relationship with Him.

## The Scenic Route

No matter how carefully we try to map out our lives, it rarely goes exactly the way we planned. A missed opportunity, death, misfortune, financial setback, divorce, or forced termination can throw us off our planned course and may force us to take more of a scenic route. Sometimes we'll find ourselves going on a path that seems so far away from where we were trying to go initially. If we are on some type of self-imposed timetable, we'll begin to panic. We'll wonder if we will ever get to where we want to go. We'll feel stuck on a path that leads nowhere while others seem to speed uninterruptedly down life's highway.

Sometimes God will have us take the scenic route, much like He did the Israelites on their journey to the Promised Land. Physically, it should have taken them about two weeks to get there from Egypt. It took forty years because God knew they weren't ready. The entire generation, though they had witnessed amazing miracles, had also endured years of slavery. Their bodies had been set free, but their minds were still enslaved. They had numerous incredible reasons to trust God's sovereignty, guidance and provision, but they doubted it the entire way.

It can be difficult to trust God as we navigate new phases, new wildernesses, and new platforms. By nature, human beings cling to things that are familiar. Few people in this world are really adventurous, especially when it comes to matters of great consequence. Most of us don't plan with a lot of room left for God to surprise us. God, however, will allow life to take room from our original plans. Just because the circumstances of life don't go the way we planned doesn't mean they're not going the way God planned.

I spoke with one of my students the other day. He wants to become a successful artist and songwriter, as do most of the kids in Columbia College's music department. All his energy, anxiety, and passion are aimed at becoming what he believes I am. I had to tell him, though, while I feel absolutely blessed and fortunate to have this occupation, I wasn't aiming for it. At some point, when I was in college, I felt like my life was moving further and further away from my suggested route. My promising singing group (bet ya' didn't know about that) was losing steam, private lessons weren't taking off, college tuition was getting ridiculous, and the idea of working as a church musician was becoming less fulfilling and less economically feasible. I seemed to be diverting from my plans, but I was falling right in line with His. What feels like the scenic route to our destination may be quite the direct route to God's destination for us.

When I was at my student's stage in life, I never would have seen myself teaching at my alma mater, traveling the world as an artist, and having an impact this way. So every weird turn seemed to be, at best, the scenic route to my vision. But standing on top of this early hill, I can see that the path to God's destination for me was quite direct. I'm glad I was too young and flexible to get in His way too much.

As I have gotten older, just like the rescued Israelites of Joshua's day, I have seen so many incredible feats of God in my life that I should trust Him an awful lot. I must manage my thoughts, however, or else the early twists, turns, and delays will cause me not to.

It takes a great deal of trust in the Lord to travel confidently along the scenic route of life. An inflated ego can make you feel that you should be there already and a deflated ego can make you feel you won't be able to handle the next twist in the road. But if you know God is sovereign, then you know that your route is purposeful. The confidence, resilience, patience, and wisdom you learn on the way are as important as the platform upon which you ultimately will stand. Make room for Him in your dreams and plans to show you the things He wants you to see before they happen.

## Make Room in Obscurity

This waiting and walking balance thing is not second nature to us. It's not easy. That's why God very rarely gives us huge platforms of influence to manage early in our faith walk. Instead, He will give us responsibility at a local church first.

If you have not submitted yourself to ministry with a local congregation, don't expect a worldwide public ministry to come from nothingness. That would be cruel of God to put you in the cross hairs of national principalities and demons when you have not yet dealt with the ones that oppress ushers and choir members at the local church level. No, God gives you a few talents of gold to deal with first. Then, after you have passed your classes, earned the degree, led your small group in worship, and conquered giving Him room in the little things, watch Him work in your life.

*"You have been faithful with a few things; I will put you in charge of many"* (Matt. 25:23, NIV).

I know social media has tainted our idea of success and YouTube® has corrupted our idea of what it takes to get there. But trust me, you do not want to enter the success arena until you're ready. And your peer-pressured, time-is-running-out sense of "readiness" is not what I'm talking about. Have you not noticed the short lifespan of many of celebrities, both in and out of the church? It's crazy out here! Enjoy being faithful over a few things. When you find peace in knowing that you are following His will, you also will find peace and contentment as you travel the journey of getting where you want to be. I haven't known such peace and levity since those early days of being faithful over a few things. People call them the "good ol' days" for a reason.

If you love sports and competition, it doesn't get much better than Olympic swimming. Whether it's Katie Ladecky or Michael Phelps, the power and grace professional swimmers exhibit, often winning by tenths of a second, is rivaled only by track runners. The start of the swimming race has always been interesting to me. After leaping vigorously off the diving board, they streamline—which is to go deep underwater and shoot forward for as long as they can, sometimes covering as much as a third of the track's length. Great Olympic swimmers are known for their powerful strokes at the water's surface, but they never move faster than when they are streamlining underwater.

Like Olympic swimmers, we have to value that time when we are moving beneath the waves with little external resistance, making room for God before the big break, the crazy demands, and the great success come.

Over the years, I've gotten way more questions from folks about how to be successful at music than I have on how to be good. People make brands before they have a product. They make websites before they have recorded any songs. They desire followers before they have any idea where they are going. They just can't wait to be public like the other artists and preachers and celebrities. In their pursuit, they forget the value of obscurity—of streamlining underwater. While you're streamlining, few people may know your destiny. They don't know your style. And you don't even know whether you're behind or ahead of everyone else. Streamlining in obscurity and making room for God while you're in that place results in meaningful and lasting growth of your craft and character.

Obscurity is where David was after he was anointed as king, tending to sheep for his dad—streamlining. Obscurity is where Joseph was after his incredible dreams only yielded a cool gig as property manager at Potiphar's house—streamlining.

Obscurity is where Esther was as she obediently followed Mordecai's teachings to gain the crown of Persia. Obscurity is often at your local church where you play and sing and preach for free before a congregation of two or three gathered in His name. Obscurity is that beautiful time where the audience is small, the pressure is light, and the calling is fun. But way too often, people who have been deceived by edited, filtered, doctored representations of success rush to the crowded surface with underdeveloped faith, undeveloped ideas, and personal brands, just so they can have some of those representations themselves. They float to the top, toward the roar of the crowd, until they realize they are flailing their arms for their "followers." They move slower, get tired quicker, and watch others who glided underwater emerge in better shape.

On the surface, you can hear everyone's opinion, you sense everyone's position, and you fight everyone's tradition.

Their approval or disapproval makes you throw away songs, trademark a name you'll never use, and invest in something that will be irrelevant a year from now.

Learn to make room for God in your obscurity.

We often put so much pressure on ourselves to be perfect immediately and available for public pageantry and fandom. God shouldn't have to compete among all those public, self-serving desires. We lose our essence and beauty by making room for public opinions and taking room from God's truth. Now that your dreams are still unrealized, and the world can't speak to them, make room for God to speak into them. Enjoy obscurity. Enjoy not being known. Enjoy the job that is just making ends meet for now. Enjoy having ample time to pray, think out of the box, and make music all night. Enjoy dealing with the outrageous folks at your neighborhood church. Enjoy the light resistance underwater. Little do you know, you are moving faster now than you ever will. You're streamlining!

You see the top of the staircase before you get there. Your eyes climb the mountain before you do. Even when the vision is in sight, your feet still have to conquer and establish themselves with every step. I'm grateful for the Grammy nomination and the opportunity to travel the world with my music all year. But I'm even more grateful that I can look back and see the unlikely journey to this point that, as far as I was concerned, was just me handling the little in front of me and God connecting the dots. I played the organ until I was confident enough to sing. Then I sang until I could study singing, and I studied until I passed the classes. I kept taking and passing classes until I could get to the summer breaks and record music. And I recorded music until God caused someone to take notice.

In between classes, but especially during the summers off, I recorded music on a little $800 ProTools starter kit from the local Guitar Center music store with a plywood and mattress foam vocal booth I built. My primary objective was to handle grades and navigate college life without a baby or too many crazy stories. My secondary objective was to work on my craft. I've failed at a lot of things—including escaping college without some crazy stories—but one thing I succeeded at was being faithful over the few things God had given me. I showed up to my worship leader gig on time, knew all the songs, prayed and studied scriptures relevant to the music and the church's vision. I took care of my home church and took pride in the little equipment we had. I passed my classes, and the one I didn't pass, I took again. I maintained my scholarships and applied for more. I worked with the school's gospel choir. I kept my '94 Ford Taurus in good condition. I paid my tickets and changed the battery. And in the midst of the crazy college story making, I held on to my faith—though sometimes weakly—and the identity God was building in me. That's all I had to be faithful over. But it's not about how much you have; but rather, what you do with what you have.

God taught the hard lessons. God made the music effective. God put my name in the wind. God blew my mind, with me giving Him just a little room. A little something for Him to bless.

Everyone's journey is different! I repeat, everyone's journey is different. The meantime between "faithful over a few" and "in charge of many" is unique to you. What you start with and what you end with is up to God, but your effectiveness, your peace, and contentment entirely rely on your ability to allow Him to lead you through it.

> *God, here's the little that I have. It's already blessed because it brought me to You. I'll be faithful to it, not because of the bigger that may come next, but because You gave it to me. Teach me at this level to make room for You, so that when the stakes get bigger, so will my dependence on You.*

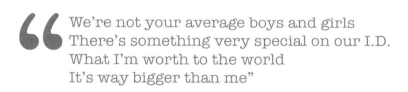

We're not your average boys and girls
There's something very special on our I.D.
What I'm worth to the world
It's way bigger than me"

"Christ Representers"
*Life Music: Stage Two*

Steeple at Big Bethel African Methodist Episcopal Church, Atlanta, Ga.

## Chapter Three
## Make Room...*In Public*

*E*very **Christian has** something to work on. Some of us have mastered smiling, speaking enthusiastically about the gospel of Jesus Christ, and sucking in our stomachs and our cuss words.

This chapter may not be for you if you're not ready to deal with that stuff in your life.

However, there is a group of Christians who pray at night, sneak into Sunday service every week, and quietly cry in the presence of God, but are a bit afraid to take Jesus too boldly outside of those four walls.

I'm not denying the power and authenticity of the secret Christian, but I believe they may be missing a significant part of their purpose on earth. Christianity practiced only in private is not a complete and authentic faith.

I'm pretty easy to spot in American airports. There aren't too many six-foot black guys walking around with a guitar case. I'm on a first name basis with the all folks at Midway International Airport in Chicago, and I'm working on that status at Chicago's larger O'Hare International Airport. Since 2014, I've flown 125 times a year, and while airplanes can present a lot of surprises, the folks in the airport rarely do. I get the same question from flight attendants: "Are you going to play for us?" Passersby ask, "Is that a bass?" because they don't peg me as an acoustic guitar player. Then there's the annoyed look people give when my case fills up the overhead bin.

What comes with carrying a guitar through the airport mirrors the experience of carrying Christianity publicly.

To the flight attendants, I politely say "No." They don't mean anything by it. Their concept of musicians is just narrow. To them, our worth lies in our ability and willingness to perform at the drop of a hat. They may appreciate the finished product, the demonstration, and the style, but they have no clue how deeply it runs—how much time I spend working on my craft, writing songs, and that I probably just had a show a few hours prior.

The way people relate to us musicians is enthusiastically limited. I've become accustomed to this as I carry my faith. To many, Christianity—especially within the charismatic recesses—has been reduced to a style, a genre, or a gimmick. From that unforgettable James Brown church scene in *The Blues Brothers* movie to the many caricatures of tongues speakers, priests, and sappy worship leaders in pop culture, Christians must contend with some established stereotypes from among the masses. That's why we need you! We need you to make room in public! Your swagger, your style, and your testimony add roundness, character, and authenticity to the image of Christianity in the world.

To passersby, my guitar case could contain anything from an electric guitar to a big violin, or a little cello to a bass. Add the fact that I'm a young black guy, and no one's first guess (except of course another guitar player) is that I'm carrying a Taylor or Martin acoustic guitar across the globe. (Not a racist thing, just a case-ist thing.) In the religion case, in America we are often bundled with Muslims, Jews, and most problematic, other Christians that do everything except reflect Christ. "No, it's not a bass, it's an acoustic guitar." And "No, I'm not simply religious, I have a relationship with the one, true living God." It's annoying, but even this kind of experience can cause you to affirm who you are and strengthening your faith and your witness.

Let's be real: guitars take up a lot of space in the overhead bin and they don't allow a lot of other stuff in there with them. My guitar inconveniences people. The people sitting on the aisle with me have to put their things across the aisle. No matter how I pack it, how I set it up, how I package it, the essence, size, and magnitude of what I'm carrying will pose a problem for some folks. I catch myself apologizing sometimes—loathing the fact that I have to carry something so big—because the response to its presence was not good.

You get it.

Christianity is going to inconvenience some people. Folks are going to angrily yell, "Who's instrument is this?!" as they search for room to do, say, and feel whatever they want. But be certain that every time you show up with that big thing, people will blame you for not giving them enough room. As guitar players, we don't move anyone else's bag to make room for our own, but we certainly make sure to board early to ensure there is always enough room to accommodate our needs. (And that may require a $50 upgrade.) While the average traveler may be carrying a bag with $300 worth of clothing made of unbreakable fabric, we are carrying $3000 worth of sensitive, powerful, hand-carved wood. Definitely breakable! Likewise, you and I are carrying an invaluable, world-changing faith and the priceless Holy Spirit! There's no way I'm checking and entrusting this bag to other people's hands, only to reclaim it scratched and broken. And I'm not going to feel bad about it either.

There is a cost to your faith. Salvation is free, but discipleship is costly. Carrying your faith in public is heavy, but it's so much less than the burden of carrying your sin. In Matthew 5:16 (NRSV), Jesus says *"...let your light shine before others, so that they may see your good works and give glory to your Father in heaven."* This is just as much of a command as "pray without ceasing" or "judge not." To keep this faith secret is not keeping this faith at all. Five chapters later in Matthew 10:33 (NRSV), Jesus is recorded saying something even more grave: *"but whoever denies me before others, I also will deny before my Father in heaven."*

Understanding God's idea of how this Christian faith should spread, influence and redeem the world, you can clearly see how important making room for Him in your public life is. When He said *"I will be with you always, even to the end of the age"* (Matt. 28:20), it was in the context of public life and ministry—making disciples, teaching and baptizing. The authority that was given to Him is meant to be demonstrated through us—not just in our personal prayer closets, but in public forums, online, offline, and in front of people!

I posit that to effectively make room for God in public consists of four principles that must invade our thinking.

### Principle #1: Be Proud of Him

There's nothing to be ashamed of. "For I am not ashamed of the gospel, because it is the power of God that brings salvation to everyone who believes" (Romans 1:16, NIV). Christianity, in its fullness—its sin-hating, people-loving, Jesus-is-the-only-way fullness—is not popular. Even in America, a country where 83 percent* claim to believe in Christ, people often seem offended by biblical perspectives and standards. Regardless of the arena, the Gospel and your identity in Christ are nothing to be apologetic for. You should probably study apologetics, but a "sorry" for your beliefs is not an option. Your faith is valuable, and like my guitar, it belongs directly over your head at all times, even if it restricts what else can be stored there. Yes, Christianity disapproves of certain approaches to life. Yes, its principles are being

* Source: ABCNEWS/Beliefnet poll, July 18, 2018 (abcnews.go.com)

argued in politics and in pop culture. Yes, some people that you love, respect, and admire are on the wrong path. But whether you are shy about it or not, the truth remains the truth! Our faith rarely asks to be obtrusive or aggressive, but God's Word does say *"stand firm in the faith"* (1 Cor. 16:13), and be positioned like *"a tree planted by the water"* (Jer. 17:8). Never let love exclude Truth. And never let meekness dissolve into shame. God is proud of you. Be proud of Him.

### Principle #2: Give Him a Proper Introduction

*You represent Him. "I...urge you to walk in a manner worthy of the calling to which you have been called"* (Ephesians 4:1, ESV). I have, no exaggeration, about 200 Christian themed tee-shirts in my wardrobe at any given time. My social media posts prove it. I've made or commissioned some on my own, but I also have been supplied several more from the many Christian apparel companies that have sprouted in the past few years. I'm the perfect endorser though. Blessed with broad shoulders and a perfect gut for a printed message, I just love to wear them.

Some argue that it's preachy or self-aggrandizing to walk around with "We Are Christ Representers," or "God Over Money," or "I Am a Believer" plastered in big fonts on my chest. But I find those arguments are generally hypocritical, as most fashion choices are self-aggrandizing. There are far more Christians proselytizing Nike® and Under Armour® brand tees. I choose to wear Christian-themed shirts for their self-checking value. There are things I won't say because I realize how hard

I'm representing for Christ just a foot below my mouth. There are actions I reconsider, not simply because they are sinful, but also because it still may give people a wrong impression of the Church. We all want to be seen and be famous, but we resist the calling to be a "walking billboard," as Lecrae and Mali Music would call it. To make room for Christ in your public walk is to embrace the fact that you represent Him...all day long, everywhere you go. You are an ambassador and God makes his appeal through you! We know God doesn't need validation, but your life—your public life—validates your faith to non-believers. God chose you to introduce Him.

### Principle #3: All You Need Is Love

Our first job is to love. *"For God so loved the world, that he gave his only Son, that whoever believes in him shall not perish but have eternal life"* (John 3:16, NIV). The third concept is simple. God loves people! He loves us enough to have made a clear path for us to return to Him— through faith in Jesus Christ. In God's eyes, when it comes to righteousness, there is not a huge difference between Adolph Hitler and Steph Curry, Justin Bieber, and your dear old grandmother on the mother's board. The only difference is some have accepted Christ and have His righteousness while others have not and, therefore, don't have a claim to His righteousness. Other than that, we are all bags of flesh open to the same manifestations listed in Galatians 5. That racist you read about, that scandalous preacher you hear about, and that drugged-up celebrity you laugh about is no less redeemable than you were. No matter how much that movie got you worked up about white people or how strange an alternative lifestyle seems to you, they are not judged by the love and compassion you show them—you are. Read what Jesus said to the Pharisees who self-righteously showed contempt toward others (Luke 18:9–14). Show love just for love's sake. Teddy Roosevelt is credited for first saying, "No one cares what you know, until they know that you care." Bold love makes room for the gospel to be shared and the gospel makes room for lives to be changed.

## Principle #4: Be a Living Message

The world is your pulpit and your life is your sermon. "For we are his workmanship, created in Christ Jesus for good works, which God prepared beforehand, that we should walk in them" (Eph. 2:10, ESV). Someone once said, "Preach the Gospel at all times, and when necessary, use words." At my home church, New Original Church of God in Christ, we still observe the tradition of testimony service. There, people volunteer to stand in front of the congregation and testify to the goodness God has recently shown toward them. I remember one evening long ago, Sister Kysel stood up and told the small gathering of her conversation with a co-worker. In their dialogue, Sister Kysel credited the Holy Spirit and trust in God for her peaceful personality and notable ability to deal with stressful situations. The final and most memorable question the co-worker had asked was, "How do you even know that God is real?" Sister Kysel responded, "Well, for one, we're having this conversation." She had connected this God-glorifying, Jesus-promoting conversation to God's sovereignty. He navigates and orchestrates seven billion lives every day, so the salvation of one brings about the salvation of another. Sure, your public witness falls on many deaf ears and several eyes are always rolled at my Christian tees. Nevertheless, the one or two who inquire about your faith because of that witness reveals more of God's purpose for your life than anything you've done within the walls of the church building; anything you have done to make money; or anything you have done to get noticed. You may not be fit for the pulpit, but you're fit for the seat you occupy and your congregation might be sitting next to you.

## Using Who You Already Are

As an artist, I've learned to be myself while representing Christ. God has always given me the grace, endurance, and anointing to navigate the public forum. I never shift to some churchy alter ego or act out of character to show God's qualities and my (sometimes wavering) allegiance to Him. I've loved t-shirts since my Forever 21® shopping days—before I turned 21—so, it was a natural move to change brands, from H&M® to H-I-M. I have always been a jokester, half charming, half recluse. That's who I am, and God uses who we are to accomplish His will. All those characteristics can be redeemed and used to persuade someone to give God a chance. My face—with its debatable handsomeness and its painful blemishes—speaks to one, or attracts another. It is my job to focus the attention I get to the faith I have.

Look at the Apostle Paul. He vigorously persecuted Christians before his conversion. Then, he used that same intensity to vigorously pursue the cause of Christ. God uses our personality—who we are and what we have. He just wants us to change brands and use it for Him.

If you're a loud, talkative person. Don't shut up, just change the subject of your conversations. Let God turn obnoxious into audacious. Aim for controlled, meaningful boldness every time you open your mouth in public.

Don't feel bad that you have supermodel beauty. Let every man that is enamored by your beauty be confronted by your Father standing alongside you and convicted by the Holy Spirit within you. God will show off your beauty, when you show off His Kingdom.

If you are quiet, let your smile, your helpfulness, and your patience speak loudly. I've observed that some shyness is a God-given personality. The great power in that personality type is demonstrated in meekness, humility, and self-control. The great concern is that these personality types are more likely to yield to the spirit of fear as well. Decide whether shyness or the spirit of fear is keeping you from lifting your hands, asserting your faith to your friends, or approaching the podium confidently. God has great public plans for the introvert that includes conquering the strongholds that contributed to being an introvert in the first place.

If fashion means a lot to you, surrender it to God. Look for ways your attire can point to Him and limit the ways they point only to you. People get very sensitive about fashion because it is a primary way we express ourselves to the world. When that self-expression is not yielded to the principles and purposes of God, however, it becomes self-worship—the elevation of your creations over your Creator. Our generation has been disappointed by how previous ones have looked good on the outside but were found to be troubled on the inside. We have compensated by spending even more time on outward appearances while arguing that immodesty, vanity, and worldliness on the outside say nothing about our hearts. Well, it does. While you focus on the development of your character do not be deceived that appearances don't matter.

You're a leader! A family, a world, and a culture changer. Act like it! Don't let something on the outside cover the beauty of what's on the inside.

Always consider 1 Cor. 8:9–11. Keep in mind that while a debate over eating foods sacrificed to idol gods motivated this scripture, the spirit of the warning can apply to fashion choice, word choice, and most any choice we can make that influences the others around us. You may be able to intellectually justify your choices, but if your freedom entices others to bondage, you are not making enough room for God in your public life.

*"Be careful, however, that the exercise of your rights does not become a stumbling block to the weak. For if someone with a weak conscience sees you, with all your knowledge, eating in an idol's temple, won't that person*

*be emboldened to eat what is sacrificed to idols? So this weak brother or sister, for whom Christ died, is destroyed by your knowledge"* (1 Cor. 8:9–11, NIV).

Wow! It's hard to believe that you, a believer and Christ representer, could severely hurt someone else's chances at getting to Christ. But it is true, you can. If I could only press one thing into your head and drive a screw into each corner, it would be that you—we—carry the responsibility of the Body of Christ's image and functionality. Sure, Christ is the Head of the Church and true unity comes in the Spirit, but individually and corporately we must make room for the Spirit to lead! You are just as much a part of how people see Christians as Bishop So-and-So. No longer can we sit our crosses down to criticize how everyone else carries theirs. Every decision you make—every facial expression, every post, every conversation—can lead someone to Christ or make them stumble.

So if they used to hear you swear, let them now hear you pray. If they saw you dancing in the club before, show them your new dance of praise dedicated to God. If you are enthusiastic about your favorite sports team, demonstrate a greater energy for His Word and His works. Take pride in publicly reading your Bible, as you did in publicly reading a *New York Times* bestseller. Replace some of your tweets about the realities of racism in a post-racial society with comments about spiritual realities. If quick, petty insults seem to easily roll off your tongue, pray that God gives you a more constructive forum for all that wit and brilliance.

Your public life is a major part of your calling on earth. If God is getting the glory only in your closet, there is a huge problem, especially if you have social media followers and you are always the life of the party. We don't live outwardly in hopes of anyone's approval, but we do live in the awareness that our world needs us to be certain and confident in our faith.

............

As I walk down the jet bridge to board a plane, the conversations my guitar attracts aren't all bothersome. Now that I have successfully gotten past the gate agent, passengers realize that I really am bringing this big guitar on board. Every so often, another guitar player—either one who checked his instrument or left it at home—questions, "So they actually let you bring that with you? I didn't think you could carry that on!"

I proudly reply, "Yes, I always carry it. I'd have it no other way." Like lugging my guitars around, carrying this Gospel is an honor, a privilege, a platform, an influencer, a weight, a nuisance to some, a threat to others, a sacrifice, and a bit of a spectacle. But I am, as you are, absolutely built, purposed, and charged to carry it on every trip.

" How can I repay You
For a whole lifetime of grace
Your love don't stop on Sunday
Even when I stop my praise."

"Got My Love"
*Life Music: Stage Two*

## Chapter Four
## Make Room...*In Private*

*W*hat happens in church on Sunday can certainly be a catalyst for change through the week, but more often, what happens during the week determines what happens and doesn't happen on Sunday. Jesus confirms that this is the way God wants us to do it: "But when you pray, go into your room, close the door and pray to your Father, who is unseen. Then your Father, who sees what is done in secret, will reward you" (Matt. 6:6, NIV).

Unfortunately some people, including me, are a lot better at consistently making room for God publicly than making room for Him to work privately. Some of us work in ministry and pray and sing before huge crowds of people, but we forget to refill our emptied-out souls through private devotion with God.

Jesus poured and healed and taught everywhere He went. He was God in the flesh, yet He still had to go "a stone's throw away" in Luke 22 to nurture Himself privately. He went away to be strengthened for His return to the crowds of people who sought healing and wisdom and forgiveness.

Power demonstrated publicly usually is accumulated privately. To be without a private relationship with God is to be unplugged from your Power Source, operating on whatever power you have within and with no more coming. It's like those night lights that are designed to work during a power outage. When the power goes out, they'll work for hours, or even days. But to keep working, they eventually have to reconnect to a power source.

Months ago, I sat with a friend as I tried to explain the fatigue that I had been working through for years. At this point, I was touring and planning yet another a tour, teaching at Columbia College, working on new music, contemplating this book, brainstorming on the next fundraiser for my nonprofit organization, blogging, and redoing my website. She posited that perhaps I had bitten off more than I could chew. That's the simplest answer, and for a moment I pondered if I was in fact just doing too much. Admittedly, my mind works in a strange manner and in that moment, it jumped to an image of a Tesla®, the premier electric car. For the longest I've wanted one because unlike most cars, it's built to go for longer distances without reliance on fuel. There's a disadvantage to having this special feature, though. While most cars can be refueled at any of the 168,000 retail locations in the US, Tesla owners have about twenty times fewer options to refill while on the road. For any extremely long road trip, a Tesla driver must map out where to fill up or otherwise end up stranded in a beautiful car that can't go any further. I've found myself at or near that point a few times in life simply because I planned out my road trip but did not consider how I would refill. And the best place to recharge a Tesla? At home.

Home is also the best place for a Christian to recharge.

Making room for God in your private life is essential. While Jesus admonishes us to "let our light shine," it must never be done for your own validation or glory. Such people are like the Pharisees of Jesus' time, which moved Him to also say: *"And when you pray, do not be like the hypocrites, for they love to pray standing in the synagogues and on the street corners to be seen by others. Truly I tell you, they have received their reward in full"* (Matt. 6:5, NIV). Our purpose is tied to what we contribute to the public, but our reward is tied to how we honor him in our private life. I'd like to explore two areas of this private life I believe we all can address.

## Private Devotion

Martha was a good friend of Jesus, but their first meeting didn't start off so smoothly. Martha invited Jesus into her house for a meal. Great!

I remember dancing, praying and rubbing "blessed oil" on all the doorways when I moved in to my new condo. I definitely invited Jesus in. I worked hard to make it a welcoming place, just like Martha did for their family Friend.

Shortly after Jesus got to her and Mary's home, Martha got "distracted with serving." She knew it was important to invite

Him in, and she knew it was important to serve Him, but she forgot to just spend time with Him. On the other hand, Mary stopped doing tasks to just listen to Him. Her attention wasn't just to the things of God, but to God himself. As Christians, we must never get so preoccupied with representing God to the masses—planning church skits, putting out gospel albums, handing out tracts, and creating Christian tees—that we forget the most basic part of Christianity: a relationship with Christ.

Outside of a relationship with Christ, Christianity will devolve into just another religion; just a brand or an approach to life. That's not what this thing is. Christianity is not just a set of cool stories, admirable standards, and something inspirational to do on the weekend. The Bible says if we draw near to Him, we will draw near to us. Biblical Christianity says *"....if you remain in me and I in you, you will bear much fruit; apart from me you can do nothing"* (John 15:5, NIV). Real Christianity is minimized when it is regarded by believers as just another religion like Islam, Buddhism, and even Judaism. A Christian's primary concern in life is cultivating an intimate relationship with God that leads to right thinking and living. This personal and often private advancement is the most integral element of this faith and your life.

My good friend and world-renowned worship leader Tasha Cobbs-Leonard astounded me with an ad-lib that I'm sure many would gloss over. In her song "Happy," as she beautifully croons, "Everything I do is about this relationship!" It's an "Aha!" moment. Everything we do must submit to the fact that we have a relationship with God. Career, marriage, dates, even service in church must work around the construction of our relationship with Him.

There are several self-proclaimed experts on the subject of prayer, but some are authentically so. I am not a prayer expert, but I can tell you what I know. First, if there is any doubt whether you should pray, the answer is littered all over the Bible—a resounding Yes! Romans 12:12 (NIV) says, *"Be joyful in hope, patient in affliction, faithful in prayer."* We're further commanded to "pray without ceasing" (1 Thess. 5:16–18), and in Matthew 6, Jesus shows us how to do it in the Model Prayer.

Make sure prayer is something you do anywhere, everywhere, and constantly—on your knees at night, in the morning when you open your eyes, while driving to work, when you eat a meal, and before you have a difficult conversation. You get to know who you talk to and prayer is how we talk to God. The world reduces prayer to "talking to the air," but then the same world constantly offers proof that we need it. Social media is a cesspool partially because the need for prayer motivates millennials and centennials everywhere to rant online. Instead of sharing every thought and care online, how different would social media be if people would first talk to Jesus? The need for guidance, the expression of our plight, the questions in our heart are human, God-given traits. Prayer—more accurately, communication with God—is designed to address that. Not your online following.

**Talking to the Air**

I am an extremely analytical person. The charismatic expressions of worship (shouting, running, crying, speaking in tongues, or any type of moving at all) never came easy to me. And praying? Well, it felt (and sometimes still feels) like I'm just talking to the air. I'm always expecting some sort of chill up my spine. I quickly open my eyes to see if an angel has shown up. Sometimes I attach this air-talking to feeling; and that's not prayer. But then, when I really need it, when someone is dying or I need an answer for real, I attach some faith and hope to that air-talking and my body is no longer looking for a tingle. My eyes don't start looking for an apparition. My soul seems to search a different land. There, my words are necessary but inadequate, and at the end of the prayer, I just hope God understood whatever I've just said.

God loves us so deeply and wants intimate communication with us so much that He even made provision for us during the times when we can't even utter words in prayer. Paul assures believers in Romans 8:26 (NIV) that, *"In the same way, the Spirit helps us in our weakness. We do not know what we ought to pray for, but the Spirit himself intercedes for us through wordless groans."*

For me, it's really prayer when I didn't articulate it very well or when I said it better than I could have in my own strength or intelligence. The fact is, until we attach faith to it, prayer really is talking to air. Prayer is religious, but when we interject faith, it becomes desirable and sensible communication with our Creator.

Unfortunately, for many of us it takes someone on their death bed or some incredibly dire situation for us to attach real faith and hope to our prayers. I'll admit, when things are good or manageable, my prayers can be shallow. For some reason, I'll run to God in sorrow more quickly than I'll run to Him in joy or serenity. I found it ridiculous that life would almost have to break my heart, stress me out, and literally bring me to my knees before I'll pray.

That's why one day after a shower I wrote this:

I don't need another tragedy
Just to realize how much I need you.
I don't need a girl to break my heart,
Just to realize where true love starts...
You've got my full attention."

"Full Attention"
*Life Music: Stage Two*

Prayers can be full of profundity, pride, performance, and piety. Prayer can be beautifully poetic, but without including what we really need—humility, faith, a broken spirit, and a contrite heart—those are just pretty words. That takes more than just thinking out loud. Most often it takes a life pause, steadying your mind and body, and truly devoting time to speak and listen to God. Otherwise, we restrict ourselves to listening for God's voice only within the context of loud, emotional, corporate worship services where we may certainly feel Him, but may not always hear Him.

God may not always choose to speak to us in the banging of drums and the screaming of the organ. The instruments celebrate His presence and illustrate His glory, but we must look for the still, small voice underneath it all to truly hear from God concerning our individual lives.

*"And he said, Go forth, and stand upon the mount before the LORD. And, behold, the LORD passed by, and a great and strong wind rent the mountains, and brake in pieces the rocks before the LORD; but the LORD was not in the wind: and after the wind an earthquake; but the LORD was not in the earthquake: And after the earthquake a fire; but the LORD was not in the fire: and after the fire a still small voice"* (1 Kings 19:11–12, KJV).

If your faith walk depends exclusively on Sunday charismatic corporate blowouts, you may be seeing the effects of "the Lord passing by." But I pray you don't miss the still, small voice that comes after the wind, earthquake, and fire. That voice is often not pursued after we just cried in the wind, shouted to the beat of the earthquake, and ran laps around the fire. There is a private, "quiet place, far from the rapid pace" where we must pursue what may turn out just to be our big God's small voice. No chills, no tears, no fainting— possibly—just talking and listening to my heavenly Dad.

## Private Obedience

Few believers I've met are overly proud of their private lives. We are all so aware of our personal failures—those times when we do what we shouldn't do, think what we shouldn't think, say what we shouldn't say, and even those times when we don't do what we should have done. I'm guessing that knowledge of most of these slip ups don't directly reach the public eye. No one knows everyone you've slept with, how many times you've lied, how many times you've browsed the dark corners of the Internet, and how many times you've wished doom to someone's career just so they wouldn't be better than you. Most casual sexual encounters don't result in babies or diseases, most drinking doesn't lead to alcoholism, and most gossip never leaves the house. Others will never know the totality of the things you do apart from God's will. And I believe God may even provide an extra layer of grace to protect the ministry He's invested in you.

He's not protecting your sin; He's protecting His investment in you to accomplish His purposes. But at the end of the day, what "they" don't know—the things done in the dark—God knows, and so do we.

I'm sure you don't need too much enlightenment on how God feels when we don't observe modesty, purity, and self-control in our private lives. I'm sure you know that our actions can literally cause the Holy Spirit to grieve. I'm sure you know that grace is not a license to sin, but rather, power to live in a righteous manner. I'm guessing you understand that no amount of sinful behavior will exceed the amount of grace available to us. Theoretically, the doctrine of eternal security means we can do practically whatever we like and still be saved.

I'm hoping you also realize, however, that a person redeemed by Jesus Christ is committed to live according to what He loves. We can't earn our salvation or maintain it, but we can confirm it. Our lives prove the change.

Our actions and attitude confirm our faith.

Our pursuits prove the conversion. All we can do with salvation is need it, receive it, and prove it. And we aren't proving it to people; often we're just testifying to ourselves that our faith and our salvation is legit.

*"...make every effort to supplement your faith with virtue, and virtue with knowledge, and knowledge with self-control, and self-control with steadfastness, and steadfastness with godliness, and godliness with brotherly affection, and brotherly affection with love. For if these qualities are yours and are increasing, they keep you from being ineffective or unfruitful in the knowledge of our Lord Jesus Christ. For whoever lacks these qualities is so nearsighted that he is blind, having forgotten that he was cleansed from his former sins. Therefore, brothers, be all the more diligent to confirm your calling and election, for if you practice these qualities you will never fall. For in this way there will be richly provided for you an entrance into the eternal kingdom of our Lord and Savior Jesus Christ"* (2 Peter 1:5–11, ESV).

Because the world is not trying to walk by the Spirit and it seems a lot easier to live according to our unchecked feelings and desires, we often ask questions such as, "Can I be saved and do this?" or "Am I going to hell because I do this?" Such questions are unfit for a believer because they minimize the significance of grace and confine salvation to a Christian's end, when salvation is also a Christian's beginning. Being saved starts your new life. It is a status that we are no longer working toward and considering once attained by the grace of God and the sacrifice of His Son. It is who you are now, and your decisions should be determined by the fact that you are saved, not just that you may be in the future.

 And if it's God that I'm after,
I just can't serve two masters.
And before something happens,
I gotta turn it all around.
Because I know
I can't just have my cake and eat it too.
'Cause it's real easy to stay on the fence
And still do you.
And it'd be cool if we could love the Lord
And still go do our thing,
But see it doesn't work like that.
You gotta be white or black."

*"No Gray"*
*Life Music*

Private obedience, the personal pursuit of righteousness, is to our benefit, but not because our salvation depends on it. Chances are your public façade will hold up for a while, even when your private life is a mess.

What sin does is a lot more insidious than yielding public exposure, unwanted pregnancies, and tainted reputations—though the public effects of private sin are real and need to be considered. The Church may not speak enough about the wart sin exacts on our hearts and minds.

Discipleship carries with it certain behaviors and actions. We should obey God because we trust and believe in Him, not just because we're afraid of going to hell if we don't. That's not the best way to live out our faith. You can mop your floor with soapy socks on your feet, but it's not the best way to get things done. You can do practically anything and make it to heaven, but that doesn't eliminate the cold truth of reaping and sowing. Earthly actions have earthly consequences. Contracting a STD or a bad reputation from promiscuous sex won't keep you out of heaven, but you still have to live with the results of what your actions reap on earth.

Sin changes us, just like being free from sin changes us. In sin, our doctrine changes to equivocate and accommodate our actions. Our minds reconsider the veracity and the necessity of the faith. We feel less inclined or allowed to pursue our relationship with a holy God, so we opt for religious validation instead. We look to pop culture to take some of our guilt away, making Christianity part of a world debate rather than a faith set apart from the world. We normalize certain sins and sinners but demonize others. We start and continue relationships that comfort our flesh but starve our spirits. That's what sin does! It hinders, it blinds, it taints, it confuses, it separates, and it binds.

Christianity does not encourage the duplicity that goes on in the American church; sin does! Sin that is covered by grace can still affect your mind, dull your senses, and render you *"ineffective and unproductive in your knowledge of our Lord Jesus Christ"* (2 Peter 1:8, NIV).

Even private sin threatens my peace and sanity. The Holy Spirit testifies to my soul that I am a child of God (Rom. 8:16); meanwhile, sin does its best to intercept that message.

So, while my singing voice doesn't change, my writing gifts don't diminish, and my reach seems only to get broader, the man off the stage feels further and further from the God he represents and the joy and the contentment God provides.

The beauty of God's grace is that when we sin, Jesus has our back in heaven (1 John 2:1) and we can always find solace in repentance. Comfortable, continual sin, however, altogether wars against our identity as saved children of God. For a second, stop searching for an answer to "Will I go to hell if...?" and consider the worrisome fact that your heart still wonders if eternity in hell is still a possibility for you at all!

Ultimately, private disobedience, rather than making room for God, puts distance between us and Him. Right now ask God (as I am) to help you prove your salvation, your new identity, to yourself with a changed and improving private life. The evidence of your change—the Spirit living inside of you—is His fruit (see Gal. 5:22–24).

 You'll know that all is forgiven
Because He'll help you to do better."

"Better"
*Make Room*

Private devotion and private obedience are not meant to be loud, but they often prove to be deafening. That private relationship you have with the Creator of the universe will give you peace, direction, and confidence in this crazy world. Don't miss out on what He has for you.

Make room for Him in private.

**"** I can't always talk to my friends
'Cause they've got expectations
That I may or may not be living up to.
I really need to rid myself of the
pressure..."

"Pressure"
*Life Music: Stage Two*

*Chapter Five*
# Make Room...*In Your Circle*

**O**n the few Sundays I'm in Chicago, but after a long week elsewhere, I must confess, I don't feel like getting up in the AM for Sunday service, so I generally elect to attend the 1:30 p.m. service at New Life Covenant Church with Pastor John Hannah. It's an incredible, energetic couple of hours decelerated only by the occasional dedication ceremony for the church's new babies. After praying for the baby and the parents, a minister prays for the baby's community—the grandparents, uncles, aunts, parents close friends, etc. During this, normally around ten family members and friends are told to encircle the young child and often young parents as Pastor Hannah and other ministers pray for them. I imagine this can be an encouraging experience for the new parents as they are surrounded by the people who promise to support them, inspire them, challenge them, and join them in rearing their beautiful gift.

I imagine it also could be discouraging.

As uncles, college friends, best friends, church friends, godparents and grandparents stand around them, I wonder if those parents realize that they can only go as far as this circle will allow them. And if there is no room for God in that circle, they can expect that their gift—the new baby—is in danger.

There's a reason why they form a circle. It surrounds the young family. Like playwright August Wilson's *Fences*, circles protect things and people by keeping them in, and they also keep things and people out. At best, a circle gives you a safe place to hide and refuel during times of chaos. When everyone in the circle is like-minded and their goals align with God's, you can't help but consider God in your decisions. The climate within a circle doesn't have to reflect the world outside. Good, godly circles act like greenhouses for what you are trying to grow—keeping the cold air out but letting the sunlight in. Good circles try to keep the negative words, ideas, and the pressure to conform away from you (because they aim to keep it away from them also), but they still know how to let God influence and develop what you have been given. People in your circle can even babysit—staying vigilant over your gift, even when life or rest temporarily calls you away.

On the other hand, as the pastor is praying for your community and all you see are people who don't filter negativity, don't allow the Light in, and can't be trusted to help develop your "baby," you're in trouble.

My friends are incredible. We are all flawed for sure. We have certainly sinned and fallen short of being good

Christians and even good friends at times, but our saving grace is how we know to make room for God. We know Who to credit for good times and Who to seek during bad times. We understand that our best, first, and last resort is a recipe of prayer, worship, and godly wisdom. I live-streamed my twenty-seventh birthday get-together. It wasn't incredibly celebratory, for I was certainly feeling the crunch of life, the pressure of my music career, everyone's expectations, and a quiet detachment from God and the Body of Christ. So, we didn't celebrate over cake and candles; instead, we sat in my den and worshiped God! In my squad, there are prophets, artists, preachers, and just about every other vocation; but in that moment, I couldn't be helped by their gifts. I would only be helped by their ability to make room, attractive and inviting room, for God. Thank God for my circle!

There's a misconception that Christianity is a religion primarily practiced in isolation. In the previous chapter, we discussed the importance of our private devotion—the time we spend alone with God. But that doesn't mean our faith is to be lived in isolation or without the comfort and support of other believers.

People sometimes can take an understandable but overrated "just-me-and-Jesus" approach to faith, and because of that, the benefits of regular church attendance have been devalued. Our generation doesn't seem to fully appreciate the influence that our friends have on our faith. I know so many people who represent the lone believer, the lone saint, or the only individual in their group attempting to align their lifestyle with their faith. Many of them have no one surrounding them who really understands or supports, so their ability to produce fruit wavers. It's like a flower trying to grow and blossom but it's being choked down by weeds.

It is simple: being meek, moderate, modest, controlled, wise, or humble is easier when the folks closest to you are striving to live that way as well. When Paul wrote letters to the Galatian, Corinthian, and Roman churches, he was not writing to groups of Sunday congregants that otherwise had little interaction. No, these were communities—extended circles of like-minded people who were unified by a faith lived daily. His teachings weren't centered on how to conduct church services, but rather, how to make room for God as a circle of believers—in grace, love, forgiveness, encouragement, wisdom, and morality.

Get it? You need godly friends! You can't afford to hoard ungodly associates in your circle. In Acts 2, the economic needs of believers were met by others within the circle. In 1 Thessalonians 5, emotional needs were met by the community. In Acts 1, they provided spiritual support. In Galatians 6, they provided accountability. God often meets your needs through the people around you. But if He only has the ear of your Sunday morning prayer circle, the enemy has six and a half days worth of friendships to work with to keep those needs unmet.

## Friend Effect Snow

In a previous chapter I mentioned the frigidity of Chicago winters. Each year, we certainly will have had our share of snow accumulation by the time March is over and spring reappears. Like any other northern American city, we can see a winter storm system approaching us from the west and we brace ourselves for what the natural flow of things will bring. But few major cities have Chicago's problem known as "lake effect snow." The passing winter storm is elongated, and accumulation is worsened simply because of our proximity to Lake Michigan. Days after the real storm has passed, we are still in white chaos simply because of the body of water nearby.

Maybe you're suffering from "friend effect snow." Hmmm… let's see. How much of what you go through is simply the result of life in your environment and how much is aggravated by who and what you are close to? How many of your thoughts, your ideas, and your beliefs are corrupted by the company you keep? How many times have your friends produced the storm that's making your life miserable? No matter how solid Chicago is, it is regularly affected by the water beside it. And no matter how much you pray, go to church, read your Bible, and speak in tongues, 1 Cor. 15:33 (ESV) says: *"bad company ruins good morals."*

Your love for those friends never goes away. You can still respect them and appreciate their good attributes. Romans 12:18 (NIV) says, *"if it is possible, as far as it depends on you, live at peace with everyone."* This isn't about you putting them in heaven or hell. This is about evaluating and possibly minimizing their effect on you! For the next few months, pay close attention to how certain friends and family members affect you—especially those of you who are young in the faith, impressionable, highly analytical, or on the fence as it is. Certain debates make you doubt God. Certain conversations make you consider sin. Certain smells take you back to your old life. Certain sights, as you scroll through your phone, lure you away from the godly lifestyle you've been pursuing. How is their presence hitting your senses? I pray the Holy Spirit causes their actions to be magnified, their words to be amplified, and the red flags be raised so you can see clearly how they fit or don't fit in God's plan for your life. At the very least, as you walk right and they walk left, you will find that your arms aren't long enough to continue to hold hands.

## Jesus: Friend or Follower

Consider John 15:15. Jesus says to His disciples, *"No longer do I call you servants, for the servant does not know what his master is doing; but I have called you friends, for all that I have heard from my Father I have made known to you."* In this regard, Jesus has made room for his disciples—and by extension you and me—in His circle. He has not withheld information from us. He has allowed himself a certain transparency to these close followers. More than simply believers, these disciples now have room in Christ's inner circle. There gifts are given, purpose is confirmed, personalities are affirmed, and insight into His life is shared.

The fourteenth chapter of John demands reciprocity in this friendship with His disciples—mutuality. He then commands in John 15:4, *"abide in Me, and I in you."* It is a sad day when someone has invited you to be his friend, but you have not extended the same invitation. His insight and validation are given liberally to those whom He calls "friend," but He will call you friend only when you have accepted Him as one of yours! Jesus is quick and faithful to make room for you, but He demands ample, special, unmitigated, unthreatened, and unimpeded room for Him in your circle.

Jesus wants the guarantee that He influences you more than anything and anyone else. He cannot fit around your existing friendships. They must fit around Him—if they fit. If your significant other or your best friend forces you to pigeonhole Christ, you are putting yourself at risk. You're at risk of missing out on the beauty, power, peace, closeness, and insight that comes with being a friend of God.

I typically avoid being brand specific because by the time you read this book, some brands will be irrelevant or obsolete, but I will refer to one here. As of this writing, Facebook® is a thing. Something like 1.4 billion people have a Facebook account. During its early days, people were restricted by a 5,000-friend limit. So, as if people really had that many people they needed to keep up with, Facebook developed a way around the cap; it's called following. It is basically a one-sided friendship that allows someone to watch you without giving you the pleasure, or misery, of watching them. While I have just shy of 5,000 friends on my personal page, I have twenty or so times that many followers. I don't engage with them. I am not influenced by them, nor do I have insight into their lives, but they are certainly given a healthy dose of me every day.

Jesus wants to be a Friend, not a Follower.

We expect Jesus to follow us with His omniscience and omnipresence. And why not? He knows when we're sleeping. He knows when we're awake. We can't confuse the Savior with Santa Claus and our relationship with Him is not one-sided.

"I have no room in my inner circle, but God, please hear me when I pray. Wipe my tears, respond to my weekly worship, and stay updated on what's going on with me. Unfortunately, I don't have room to make you Friend and have insight into what's going on with you."

Blame it on the 5,000 friend limit.

We expect that God will follow us and pay attention to our issues, our convictions, and our plans without promising that we will follow His. We have turned the tables on heavenly friendship. We want God to hear our prophecies and shouts of what we call forth when we don't bother to make time to let Him influence and repurpose what we want to call forth. People walk into the church charged with a call to influence it, without even thinking that they may be the one in need of influencing. God influences the desires of our hearts, and then gives them to us. And aside from our personal world-corrupted belief system, the biggest impediments to that influence are the people around us.

Let His will be done in your circle of friends, as it is in heaven.

I don't advise that you immediately go deleting friends like you're making room for more pictures in your phone. After all, you're not dealing with megabytes, you're dealing with humanity. I wouldn't do anything too hastily, remembering that God's ways are higher than ours, and He normally has a reason for lives to intertwine. However, you must intentionally give your new significant other, your existing friends, and your #friendgoals to Him. Let Him blow your mind with His insight on who is around you. He knows how you are built, how they are built, and how you fit together. He knows when there is an opportunity for you to minister to them, and He knows when there is a chance they can hinder you.

Lay aside the weight of having to decide alone.

Make room for God in your circle! Pray for greater discernment, greater understanding of your assignment, and a little insight into theirs. Pray that their motives and their impact on you become incredibly clear. Then, pray that God gives you the right way to deal with these loved ones. Making room for God in your circle may lead to Him teaching you how to properly deal with who you keep around. Your first step may not be simply cutting folks out, but instead intentionally bringing faith to the forefront of your conversations and letting them adjust to you. Who knows, maybe they've been feeling the same way about you. Maybe they're even reading this book right now, too.

## Late Note

I had already finished writing this chapter. I'm contemplating whether I should write another section on sanctifying what we allow our ears to hear and our eyes to see. You'll see my decision soon enough. As I write this, record an album, tour, and prepare for my fifth year as a teacher at Columbia College, something even more important is happening. I'm watching my social life get...well, liposuction. That's the best way I can say it. The excess fat is being removed. No one in my life is anything less than amazing, but the weight of carrying them all was still detrimental to my health and my self-image. The heartbreak selfishness caused, the soul ties that loneliness caused, and the questioning that utter pettiness caused has weighed me down, even as I've changed my diet and run marathons with Christ.

Some things require surgery. Painful cutting. They have to be removed. It's cutting that has nothing to do with the quality of friends or associates excised; it's about you. And you don't need any special rudeness, arrogance, or indifference to carry out your surgical procedure. All you need is—all the Spirit wants you to use is—truth. The truth of who you are. The truth of who God is calling you to be. The truth of what you can handle and the truth of how they influence you. You'd be amazed at how much the truth exposes and sets your circle back to order.

Truth causes you to reflect. Honestly, maybe I liked my friends too much. Maybe I gave the wife search too much attention. Maybe I sought after human affirmation and company too heavily. Maybe I gave too much credence to their opinions. Maybe my house was tailored to entertaining my squad and not to hosting the presence of God.

Maybe it's time to make room.

**"** I recognize this is a day that you have made
So I walk in love and put a smile on my face
But in case I run into someone on a different page
Help me maintain"

"Maintain"
*Life Music: Stage Two*

## Chapter Six
## Make Room...*In Your Day*

To evade **public** school rules that would keep me out of school for another year because of my "late" birthday, my mother enrolled me in a Catholic school for a year. See, the school year started a few weeks before my birthday—before I'd be eligible to enroll in public grade school. Apparently, by the time you get to third grade, they don't care, but for two years I had to be schooled outside of the Chicago public school system. For second grade, I ended up at St. Philip Neri on Chicago's Southside. It was easily my least favorite school year for many reasons, but it gave me a different religious experience than I was used to from my Pentecostal home church. I'm pretty sure the teachers and priest at St. Philip Neri can be credited with giving me my first meaningful introduction to the Lord's Prayer. We had to learn it, likely for a grade, and in weekly mass (I think it was weekly). Someone would lead us in reciting it. I remember temptation, forgiveness, and will be done on earth. Even at six years old, I recognized the beauty of its poetry and the value of the weekly, structured communication with God. Except that weekly is not what it was supposed to be at all.

Likely referring to Exodus 16, the Model Prayer says, *"Give us this day our daily bread...."* There's nothing weekly about praying, about worshiping, or about making room for God. We must make a daily investment into our relationship with Him, perform daily calibration with His Word and plan for us, and daily make room for Him to influence and protect. In Exodus 16, the people of Israel were fresh out of Egypt, roaming the wilderness, and starving. God promised to feed them by providing manna falling like rain every morning to their camp. The condition was that they only collect what was needed for that day. Besides that, the manna was only good for one day. There was no such thing as manna leftovers.

It is His mandate that room be made for Him daily—not weekly, not annually, and not when we get around to it. Some of us only make room for God situationally—on an event-to-event or as-needed basis. Every day those Israelites went out to gather their daily bread, they had to consider the incredible God who provided it. Every day, they had to make room for God before they could even eat.

And here's the thing: God made it that way intentionally.

In Exodus, when the children of Israel gathered their bread-like substance from heaven, Moses cautioned them to gather only as much as they needed for that day. While they were in the wilderness, they needed to live in confidence that God would provide for them again the next day. But true to human nature, some people ignored Moses' instructions and gathered more than they needed. They stashed some for later. But the next morning, their stashes of manna were covered with maggots and had started to smell.

They were lazy doubters. Instead of getting fresh bread every morning, they ended up with a pantry of rotten bread—perhaps, symbolic of a rotting relationship with God. The encouragement they received the day before was already stale. Their loveless religion stank! And yesterday's faith was covered in maggots! Learn from the Israelites and don't live off yesterday's, last year's, or grandma's bread. Make room for a fresh encounter with God daily.

When the Israelites learned they could gather only enough for their daily bread, that meant each person had to trust God and consider Him daily for their sustenance. God wants a relationship with you that is renewed daily. Like day-old manna, you can't live on yesterday's sustenance. Your relationship needs to fall afresh daily.

## Good Morning, Cell Phone

I'll be honest. The first thing I think to do in the morning is not pray or sing a new morning song to the Lord. I pick up my phone and anxiously check for missed calls, unread messages, and updates and narratives social media has to offer. This hurried search through my cell phone is the first jolt of energy I get when I wake up.

If you have a similar testimony, I imagine we all should ask God how He feels about our readiness to engage in communication with the world versus our slothfulness in searching for His missed calls, unread messages, and updates.

Before you check for and return missed calls from people, check in with God. Maybe He's been trying to reach you. Daily communication with Him will keep us connected to His calls, massages and updates.

We normally awaken from five to eight hours of weird dreams, the body working to heal itself, or just plain old peaceful sleep. So many issues were created and addressed in those few hours we were dead to the world. So much happened. So many moves were made. So many spiritual schemes were developed and foiled. If we wake up to missed calls from the drama, hustle and bustle of natural life, imagine how much we have missed in the more real and eventful spiritual world. Demons and angels, saints and sinners have had us on their mind for the hours we slept. So the same way we immediately check our phones for missed correspondence, it is very important to check in with Jesus and get our marching orders, our encouragement, and a renewed perspective at the beginning of the day.

I'll save the deep spiritual warfare talk for another book and probably for another author; but be aware that what happens to you throughout the day may be significantly influenced by what went on while you were asleep. You need to check in with the Boss immediately. In addition to the chance to express gratitude for another day, I hope your morning check-in call not only helps you gain perspective on how to defeat your daily giants, but also helps you realize your role in helping others fight theirs.

If you are like me, it takes twenty minutes or so for my voice to warm up, so I tend to return missed calls only after reading the unread texts. I'm sure you can imagine where I'm going—read your Bible! For every text your phone receives, read a verse or a chapter. I know what you're thinking: "How do I just pick a Scripture passage to read?" I get it. Without a preacher's prepared sermon and directed reading, it may seem like I'm asking you to pick a wave in the ocean. Here are four easy ways to do it.

First, new Christians tend to have incredible success with this method: Pray for God to lead you to the right page, then open your Bible and start reading where you've been directed. As you read, remember: *"All Scripture is inspired by God and is useful to teach us what is true and to make us realize what is wrong in our lives"* (2 Tim. 3:16, NLT). So wherever you turn, chances are you will find something to hold on to or ask God about.

Second, believers who feel they are too mature for that method can reread Scripture passages that the preacher introduced during recent services. Preachers and teachers are human, too. They interpret things from their point of view and offer to you what they feel is a universal message from their reasonable perspective and revelation. The Word, however, has a supernatural power to speak to both the congregation and the preacher or teacher with the same text.

Personal study of what biblical revelation given in a public forum will often prove to be fruitful. It is a Christian shame when a preacher moves you to tears and applause during the worship service, but their words and biblical references are never revisited. You loved the biblical feast that was prepared for you to consume during worship, but you never retained the recipe. Your walk, then, relies totally on the preacher's offering and ability to consistently deliver. Realistically, some people like it that way because they don't want to be held responsible for their own edification and enlightenment. They want to take the preacher's word for what's in the Bible and never explore God's Truth for themselves. But Paul says, *"Study to show yourself approved as a worker"* (see 2 Tim. 2:15).

Third, if you're like me you research everything. Everything? Everything. If I don't know why I have an ache or how to treat it (with oil and apple cider vinegar), I look it up! If I can't tell you offhand how old a random celebrity is, I look it up! So, if I'm not sure how God feels about my day's events, I look it up! There have been so many times that I have searched the Internet for scripture passages relating to "impatience," or "bad day in the Bible," or "social justice Jesus."

The Internet, known for its dark corners, also includes a wealth of Christian thought and scholarship. Chances are your favorite preacher, teacher and author search Google liberally. Why aren't you? Just please be careful to pursue responsible and reasonable scholarship in your study. There are a lot of people out there teaching all sorts of things. Go to trusted sources and pray for revelation and protection in your search.

BTW, there's an app for this! There are calendars, and devotionals, and search engines, oh my! There are plenty of Bible reading plans and Bible plan enforcers out there. Invest in one! Many are free.

God is worthy of at least a free notification on your phone, right?

At the end of the day, that's precisely what it comes down to. How much room do you feel God deserves in your day? Our jobs pay us, so we conclude that they generally deserve our time and effort. Our significant others love us and address many of our basic physical and emotional needs; so we give them lots of attention, financial resources, energy, and time, simply because they deserve it. Then, it seems like every man has this incredible soft spot for his mom and is willing to take out a second mortgage to make sure she can retire comfortably because Mama deserves it! These are the kinds of things we're willing to do for the people we love and who love us.

So, if we'll do that for them, how much more can we do for the God in whom we claim to believe—the One who gives us life, orchestrates our journeys, protects, blesses, makes a way out of no way, loves, and forgives us? How much more for He who died and rose again for our sake? Nevertheless, it seems as if we make it harder for Him than for anyone else to receive the time and space to work in our lives that He deserves.

God deserves room in your day. Besides, *your* day needs *Him*!

Start piling up godless days and you'll see that you've led a godless life—simply breathing the air He gives but not receiving the wisdom and peace He reserves just for you.

You're not cheating God by not giving Him room in your day, you're cheating yourself!

Finally, I rush to my top three social media apps to check on what's happening with the world since I last opened my eyes. In about a minute I know which celebrities passed away, whose phone got hacked, who has a new album, and whether someone of renown has mentioned me. More than any generation, millennials and centennials engage in the lives of people they don't know. They invest emotional, financial, and spiritual energy to personalities far away, but neglect the world close to them. We follow our president's trending news, chide our movie stars, and defend our favorite artists more than we do the people in our immediate families and church communities.

We send our attention and love right past our inner circles to people we aren't called to—people who won't even notice. It's unlikely that we can deprogram our collective instinct to get daily or trice-daily updates on pop culture, Washington, DC, and Hollywood. But we can intentionally offer our attention to the health of our church, the status of our family members, and the condition of our sphere of influence. This way, we stay engaged with our call rather than inspecting how everyone else lives theirs.

## Just Got Saved

I've had my share of media interviews and Christian press interviews. I think I've become pretty adept at fielding the standard interview questions: "How did you start?", "How do you feel onstage?", and "Tell us something about you we wouldn't know." But there is one question, specific to Christian outlets, that always feels a little weird to answer: "When did you get saved?"

Now, being a church boy basically from birth—seriously, my mom's...ummm...water broke during Sunday morning service and I was born shortly thereafter. Still, I don't have an incredible darkness-to-light, streets-to-the-altar, hood-to-holiness testimony. I observed, respected, and even aided (as the musician) moves of God. I didn't quite understand what was happening, nor did I have a knock-down-drag-out spiritual experience myself, but I think I believed in it. I had no reason not to. I remember on numerous occasions, declaring I was saved or crying because of the highly-charged service, but could I pick out one of those as the defining moment of my Christian life? As a matter of fact, I don't feel like I added definition to my salvation until I got to college. It was there, amid the temptation of cute girls, a sketchy reputation, and social drama that I realized my life didn't appear too Christian. My lifestyle certainly was not screaming "Jesus" to anyone else, even though I sang and played His praises around the city every week. It was then I realized that our salvation can't all hinge on one churchy declaration made some time before puberty. It is determined, established and applied as we walk in the identity of the saved every day.

Jesus says in Luke 9:23, *"If any of you wants to be my follower, you must turn from your selfish ways, take up your cross daily [not just one good, histrionic time], and follow me."* That cross signifies full surrender, dying to self, and considering Christ...daily.

So, to answer the question from radio interviewer #245: "When did you accept Jesus as your Lord and Savior?" This morning. I got saved for the seven thousandth or so time this morning. When I make room for God daily, I affirm my salvation (2 Peter 1:10, my favorite passage) and stay close enough to hear the Spirit affirm that I am a son of God (Romans 8:16). What a difference a day makes!

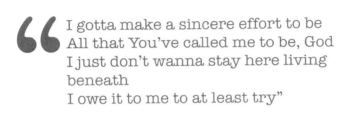 I gotta make a sincere effort to be
All that You've called me to be, God
I just don't wanna stay here living
beneath
I owe it to me to at least try"

"Try"
*Make More Room (Deluxe)*

## Chapter Seven
# Make Room...*In Your Environment*

**A**s I typed the header for this chapter, I wondered if there was a less clunky word for environment, so I queried my best friend and the smartest person I know, Google, just to see if some cooler or more precise words would populate. Somehow the click-train brought me to an article* on hypnosis. I couldn't resist. Out of that Google search, I expected some stuff about allergens, or noise pollution, or solar panels, not "You are getting sleeeeepy" talk. So, yeah, I clicked it. Because, well...you never know.

Turns out it wasn't creepy at all. I'm sure the manipulation of the principle can be troublesome, but the article's principle itself was spot on and neutral. The article discussed the power of suggestion that the mundane things in our environment have over us. For instance, the article noted that when the scent of cleaning liquid in the air, people

*Source: "How Your Environment Influences You" (www.uncommon-knowledge.co.uk)

tend to be cleaner and tidier. Or when holding a cup of hot coffee, people are most likely to describe someone as "warm and friendly." Or when a briefcase is visible, people get a bit more focused and competitive. This therapist asserted that "the environment we find ourselves in has a highly hypnotic effect on us." And in all of my holy and rightful skepticism of hypnosis, I had to agree.

Hopefully we all can admit that what we see and hear—what we sense—affects our decisions, our actions and thoughts. Churches never were equipped with spotlights, haze, and incredible sound systems until church administrators realized that spotlights direct attention, haze creates anticipation and sound systems, well, allow the preacher to be heard. The modern church, whether it is for entirely noble reasons or not, has figured out that environment matters. I've had great sets that seemingly had less impact and energy simply because of the temperature of the room.

We cannot take charge of our thoughts, avoid seeking destructive friends, and discontinuing problematic habits without doing something about our environment: Monitoring, filtering, changing—as much as we can—what we see, hear, smell, taste, and touch.

In a great interview with award-winning gospel artist Anthony Brown, a question was posed to us by someone in the audience. She asked, "How do you stop comparing yourselves with your peers?"

Now, of course, there are loftier responses like, "Remind yourself every day of your God-given purpose and learn to rest in your own divine significance." Something like that. Her question was like a fastball down the middle of the plate: it would be easy to hit it out the park. I elected to answer it a different way, though. I told her that Anthony and several others, while they are my friends, are also wildly successful. While I will always support their elevation, I must admit that constant engagement with their weekly successes makes me appreciate my own blessed situation a little less. Sure, prayer and "daily affirmations" can help, but so would deleting some social media apps, or at least temporarily unfollowing their posts. (I realize in today's culture that practice may be taboo, and many people feel that if you aren't a constant audience to their online offerings, you don't love them like you should. It's ridiculous to me, but there are still ways to limit your intake politely.) If your desire to support or your need to be in the know is killing you, feeding your flesh, and making you implode, stop!

Learn to take control of your own environment. Some smells, sights, and sounds are not outlawed by the Bible, but for your health and sanity, they should be outlawed by you! Only you can evaluate how your environment pushes you to God or pushes you to sin. Only you, directed by the Holy Spirit and permitted by humility, can observe what the smell of someone else's marijuana, the drama of your favorite TV show, and the lyrics of your favorite song really does to your heart and your head.

## Secular Music

When I was growing up, few topics were debated more in the church forum and within the individual mind. Music and entertainment are as ubiquitous as water in our lives, so it would take an incredible effort to avoid and aggressively detest every fruit of pop culture.

Broken humanity has tainted some of the good that Christians attempt to do. But also I believe the continuous efforts and influence of the Kingdom have redeemed some of what was meant for evil in this world. So today, the lines have been blurred by Christians producing music that lacks relevance, honesty, and integrity. Conversely, there's been a surprising abundance of love, creativity, and inspiration from the music created outside of the faith. Add to that the generation we serve—one that prefers autonomy, is suspicious of the Church's heart, and is influenced by celebrities, humanistic movements, and one million blogs—and you have a very difficult question to answer, defend, and apply.

Should we listen to non-Christian or non-gospel music?

The value of music in the life of a believer certainly is a topic worthy of discussion. Songs are the absolute best messengers due to their understandability and memorability. Music creates and cures moodiness, glee, discouragement and satisfaction, all while planting in our minds who and what to credit for it—God, beautiful women, a foolish man, or the "Blame it on the a-a-a-a-a-alcohol."*

* "Blame It," lyrics by James T. Brown, John Conte, Jr., Jamie Foxx, et al.

Obviously for someone developing their faith in an invisible God, amid tragedy and world immorality, the words they allow to penetrate their eardrums can make or break their experience. Let's just assume that authentic Christian/gospel music will point to Him 100 percent of the time. So does that mean music that is not from the Christian genre points away from Him? And are its effects—negative, positive, or neutral—the same from person to person?

Although the Bible was not written at a time where there was a recording industry (unless you count writing the words down), the world of the ancient Israelites still was blessed by music. They relied on music in worship, prayer, celebration, praise and lament. And if Song of Solomon is actually a song, music was a soundtrack to intimacy and love as well. Music was used for encouragement, admonishment, war, and celebration. I believe the ancient Israelites were comforted in knowing their music came from one of their own. Whether from Miriam, Asaph, or David, or one of the other musicians, they shared a common perspective, posture, and goal. Today, music has the same applications, but in a society of mixed faiths and religious attachments, it is necessary to test the perspective, posture and goal of the musicians we allow in enter our environment. To allow my songs into your home, is allowing my opinions, my beliefs, and my personality into your intimate space.

Imagine if every time you played your favorite recordings, the musicians and singers in them would immediately appear in your house. For the span of that song or album, they can talk to you, move a few things around, and make you intensely aware of their fragrance, their mood, their friends, and their lifestyle. How long could they hang around before you start feeling different about yourself? How long before you feel like falling on your knees and worshiping God? How long before you catch a contact high from their aroma? How long before you start gloating about your sexual conquests or feeling ashamed you have few to speak of? How long before you feel like you can seize the day? How long before you feel like the day has already seized you? Do they feed your love and desire for God, or do they make you crave what the world offers? Do you feel stronger in your faith or does Christianity feel less adequate? Your favorite artists influence you as much as your favorite friends. Choose them, and how you interact with them, wisely.

Some people may wish there was an explicit statement in the Gospels that instructs, "Thou shalt not listen to music not released by marketed and approved Christian artists." The question: "Is listening to secular music a sin?" is a common inquiry, but it is not the right one to ask. We are so cognizant of the immediate impact our decisions have on our sin record that we don't pay enough attention to what our decisions make room for. To create a lifestyle based on what seems to be sin and what doesn't is tough, shortsighted, and places you at the center. A lifestyle based on what makes room for God to move, bless, teach, and challenge is pleasing to Him and is rewarding and enlightening to us because it places Christ at the center.

Have fun arguing your advanced music theology next time you have your friends over, but for your own spiritual health, sanity, and benefit, take time to honestly evaluate, what room your musical selections give God to impact your environment. A room with furniture stacked up in front of the windows will let only a little sunlight in. Your music may be blocking the light of divine wisdom from entering your heart. If God had to get to you in a hurry, could you hear Him with through the music you listen to? If He had to get to your mind, would the music in your ears block out what He was saying?

Don't wait for the preacher to tell you what to do and what not to do; ultimately, it is up to you to work out your soul's salvation with fear and trembling, respect and humility. Take the initiative to be honest with yourself and make room for God in your music choices. The same goes for books, movies, and television shows. I'll never be so conservative to say anything that doesn't explicitly mention God is an abomination to my environment. But I'll also never be so liberal to say that all creativity is being used to the glory of God. Take control of your environment so that while your favorite musician sits on your couch bellowing out tunes, you can still hear Jesus on the loveseat because His voice is even louder.

## Special Spot

I mentioned earlier that on the rare Sundays I'm home, I love to attend the late service to hear one of Chicago's favorite men of God, Pastor John Hannah. I'm sure he has flaws like anyone else, but he is one man that you just know has a vibrant, passionate relationship with God. In 2010, he invited me to his church for what was my first professional opportunity to share my original music. His worship team opened the service in an amazing fashion. Excellent, zealous and sincere, I had never experienced the like. Hundreds of congregants rushed to the front of the stage, even exceeding the passion of the worship team. Somewhere, in the scrum a man was on his knees. He raised his hands to the heavens and smiled as tears ran down his face. It was Pastor Hannah.

I had never seen someone in his position be that...normal. In my experience, pastors generally were moved ten times less than everyone else in the room. Twenty minutes in, his assistant tapped him on his shoulder, gave him a tissue to wipe his face and a cordless microphone. Then, with five seconds to gather himself, he walked behind the fray and up the stage stairs.

He went on to preach a very moving message that focused on how he had tailored his home to remind him of God. I'm sure he had all the normal Christian paraphernalia—crosses, positive sayings, or whatever. But he described a certain place he'd established in a high traffic area so that whenever he stepped in it, he vowed to pray at that moment. It was a novel concept to me at that time in my life. I had hallowed areas for music, sleep, eating, game-watching, and even painting, but I hadn't declared a single inch of my house as exclusively God's. Sure, you can pray anywhere, and confining God to a certain area in your home is the complete opposite of what I want to convey here. The beauty is in the fact that Pastor Hannah had consciously and deliberately arranged his home in a way that would remind him of his commitment to God. He made room for God in his environment.

In that spirit, when I got my first sizable apartment, I set up a spot under the stairs—where Harry Potter would have slept—fully equipped with pillows, a random cross, guitar, Bible, and a Bluetooth® speaker. For a few weeks, I searched for the right background instrumental music, the right routine, until I fell out of love with the idea altogether. I blame immaturity for my inability to stick to the plan. And it's possible I turned it into an interior design project rather than a plan to make room for God in my home. But I will say that in those few weeks, my mind was on living better and doing better. I said no to compromising situations because the very walls of my house were reminding me of my purpose and relationship to God. Over time, however, that closet got filled with new art projects, coats, and anything else that didn't belong out in the open. And as that cross got covered by stuff, my life got mired in mess, too. My house started to look like my walk with Christ. It catered well to company, but not so well to Christ.

Wow, sorry...that just hit me in the heart.

I converted His space in my home into a storage closet purposed to keep the rest of my house clean for people. He had the smallest room in the place and quickly began losing that space as people, career, and my own desires for neatness took priority.

Yikes! I'm sorry God.

What I was doing to His space in my environment is what I was doing to His space in my life.

Since then, I've moved to a much bigger condo. There I've been able to dedicate a much larger room as my Jesus space. It's decorated with lights and a board for writing prayers, scripture passages and whatever else. It's lovingly decked with beanbag chairs, pillows, and carpet for marathon prayer and worship sessions to be easy on the knees and back. It's in an area where I can scream and only God would hear. It's a vast improvement from my earlier attempt at giving Him room, and evidence that part of my life is getting better, even though other parts still need work. I don't spend enough time in there, though, because every so often the light seems to turn itself on. It's as if it's beckoning me to come in and visit, reminding me of my commitment and nudging me to make some room.

## Triggers

Well, next time you have that moment, do the less righteous version of you a favor: make your environment preach to you. Establish some triggers. Set up your home, your side of the dorm room, your office, or your car in a way that they remind you of who God wants you to be and what He wants you to do. Whether it means removing pictures from your phone, hanging a sign over the bed, or dangling a cross over your rearview mirror, go as hard (be as exhaustive) as you need to! Remember, Jesus put it like this:

*"If your right eye causes you to stumble, gouge it out and throw it away. It is better for you to lose one part of your body than for your whole body to be thrown into hell. And if your right hand causes you to stumble, cut it off and throw it away. It is better for you to lose one part of your body than for your whole body to depart into hell"* (Matt. 5:29–30, NIV).

Now, I could be wrong, but I don't believe Jesus is anticipating a Kingdom of one-eyed and one-handed people. I do believe, however, that He wants to emphasize doing whatever it takes to stay in God's will and enjoying the certainty of the faith. Anything we think of will undoubtedly pale in comparison to what He already has done for us.

Our environment—the sights, the smells, the sounds—has a certain hypnotic effect on us. Knowing this, what can you do to ensure that your environment makes room for God?

" I will make room for you
I will prepare for two
So You don't feel that You
Can't live here
Please live in me"

"Make Room"
*Make Room*

## Chapter Eight
## Make Room...*Period*

**M**y plane landed with a loud and terrifying thud. It was raining profusely in Washington, DC and all of us passengers were trapped in this Boeing 737. We were sitting impatiently on the runway, just a frustrating one hundred feet from the gate. Silencing our murmurs of irritation, the pilot turned on his microphone and said, "We can see our gate. It is free, but there are several planes in our way like a puzzle. They are trying to move them out of our way. Until then, we can't proceed."

Everyone moaned in disbelief because we had done everything right. We'd boarded quickly to allow the plane to leave on schedule. The pilots had even managed to knock fifteen minutes off our flight time. Back when we started our descent, the flight attendant proudly promised we were getting into DCA early. But now that fifteen-minute cushion turned into a thirty-minute delay simply because so much was in between our plane and our gate.

What if God's peace, His favor, His mate for you, actually landed within one hundred feet of you fifteen days ago, but your tardiness, your rain delay, your inability to make room has forced it/them to just sit on the runway and wait?

I began writing this when I really hadn't made much room for God. My life had gotten consumed by doing God-oriented things—writing gospel songs, giving scholarships, defending the faith, and serving God's people. But I hadn't done much as far as our actual relationship. I barely prayed. Never fasted. Only read Scripture to win a debate. I became so disgusted by the monotony of church, I didn't realize that I was the one bringing a monotonous relationship to church. Like every album, God preached to me with this one (titled *Make Room*, go figure) just as everything I asked for and needed seemed a mere one hundred feet away. It was blocked by other aircraft that should've been long gone by now.

One day, I told my assistant that I miss the discipline I once had and that she was charged with enforcing my own schedule on me. In other words, I asked her to make sure that I made sure to make time for prayer, writing, devotion and worship every day. The next day I woke up early (for me) and before I turned the TV on I prayed. All day long I felt like some clogged runway had suddenly been opened. I was amazed that the peace, energy and joy I was lacking was not hundreds of miles away. It didn't take a year of rehab to feel His presence again. The divine hug I needed was just a short distance away. As soon as I made room with intentionality— not just fasting because it's 5:00 p.m. already and I haven't eaten all day anyway—He was right there! Now there are a few things, like a wife, that may still be miles away, but I was amazed by the answered prayers that had already arrived but were just waiting for me to make room for them.

If you know that it's been a while since you made a deliberate effort to sanctify time and energy for God, I bet there is a Blessing 737 idling one hundred feet away, refusing to turn its engines off. God pursues His children, and I can almost guarantee you haven't gotten too far to feel an immediate difference. He has done an incredible job of making room for us on earth (Genesis 1), before great people (Prov. 18:16), in His family (Eph. 2:19–22), and even in heaven (John 14:2).

Now let's prepare our hearts, clear our heads, adjust our dreams, consider our public witness, protect our private bonds, prune our social circles, schedule our days, and arrange our environments in a manner that makes room—intentional, permanent, influential room—for God, and just for Him.

## About the Author
## Jonathan McReynolds

**J**onathan was born on the Southside of Chicago in 1989, but the 2010 phenomenon that was birthed in his college dorm room amid a few friends has graduated to Christian music's biggest stage—picking up fans like Stevie Wonder, Lalah Hathaway, Kirk Franklin, CeCe Winans, Nicki Minaj, and Tori Kelly along the way. And Jonathan did it with an incredible voice and a beautifully honest approach to songwriting. That honesty is now recorded in print.

His latest full-length album, *Make Room*, debuted number one on *Billboard* Gospel (and regained the number one spot months later), and garnered an unprecedented 1.3 million streams in the first week. The album is hailed as his best work, the best album of 2018, and an instant Grammy® favorite. From this album, Jonathan earned his first number one single "Not Lucky, I'm Loved." His second album, *Life Music: Stage Two*, features superstar fan India.Arie, and remained number one on the *Billboard* Gospel chart for four weeks.

Jonathan earned a Bachelor of Music degree at Columbia College, and in May 2015, he received a Master of Arts degree in biblical studies from Moody Theological Seminary.

His contribution to society beyond the music industry is extremely important to him. Jonathan is an adjunct professor at Columbia College and an official contributor to *Huffington Post*. In 2016, he founded Elihu Nation, a nonprofit organization that promotes wisdom, and has awarded at least $10,000 in scholarships annually. In the summer of 2018, he fulfilled a childhood dream of being inducted into Mensa, the world's largest and oldest high IQ society.

• • • • • • •

"My ministry is all about being authentic and genuine, pure and transparent. That's who I try to be as a person," he reveals. "I'm direct, I'm blunt. I'm not a fan of church clichés and 'Christian-ese'. *Life Music* is concerned with showing others and reminding myself how the faith doesn't just fit every part of life but should frame every part of life."

Jonathan McReynolds